# Choose your king

## 1 SAMUEL

by Tim Chester

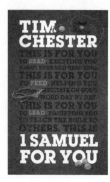

# 1 Samuel For You

If you are reading *1 Samuel For You* (see page 71) alongside this Good Book Guide, here is how the studies in this booklet link to the chapters of *1 Samuel For You*:

Study One → Ch 1-2      Study Four → Ch 7-8
Study Two → Ch 4-5      Study Five → Ch 9, 11
Study Three → Ch 5-6    Study Six → Ch 12-13

Choose your king
The Good Book Guide to 1 Samuel
© Tim Chester, 2014. Reprinted 2017, 2019.
Series Consultants: Tim Chester, Tim Thornborough,
                    Anne Woodcock, Carl Laferton

Published by:
The Good Book Company

**thegoodbook**
COMPANY

thegoodbook.com I www.thegoodbook.co.uk
thegoodbook.com.au I thegoodbook.co.nz I thegoodbook.co.in

ISBN: 9781909919594 I Printed in Turkey

# CONTENTS

# introduction: good book guides

Every Bible-study group is different—yours may take place in a church building, in a home or in a cafe, on a train, over a leisurely mid-morning coffee or squashed into a 30-minute lunch break. Your group may include new Christians, mature Christians, non-Christians, mums and tots, students, businessmen or teens. That's why we've designed these *Good Book Guides* to be flexible for use in many different situations.

Our aim in each session is to uncover the meaning of a passage, and see how it fits into the "big picture" of the Bible. But that can never be the end. We also need to appropriately apply what we have discovered to our lives. Let's take a look at what is included:

⊕ **Talkabout:** Most groups need to "break the ice" at the beginning of a session, and here's the question that will do that. It's designed to get people talking around a subject that will be covered in the course of the Bible study.

⊥ **Investigate:** The Bible text for each session is broken up into manageable chunks, with questions that aim to help you understand what the passage is about. **The Leader's Guide** contains **guidance for questions**, and sometimes ⊗ additional "follow-up" questions.

☺ **Explore more (optional):** These questions will help you connect what you have learned to other parts of the Bible, so you can begin to fit it all together like a jig-saw; or occasionally look at a part of the passage that's not dealt with in detail in the main study.

⊖ **Apply:** As you go through a Bible study, you'll keep coming across **apply** sections. These are questions to get the group discussing what the Bible teaching means in practice for you and your church. ☺ **Getting personal** is an opportunity for you to think, plan and pray about the changes that you personally may need to make as a result of what you have learned.

⬆ **Pray:** We want to encourage prayer that is rooted in God's word—in line with his concerns, purposes and promises. So each session ends with an opportunity to review the truths and challenges highlighted by the Bible study, and turn them into prayers of request and thanksgiving.

The **Leader's Guide** and introduction provide historical background information, explanations of the Bible texts for each session, ideas for **optional extra** activities, and guidance on how best to help people uncover the truths of God's word.

# why study 1 Samuel?

The book of 1 Samuel traces the history of God's people from a situation where they had no king and "everyone did as they saw fit" (Judges 21 v 25), via the rule of the king they want, to the beginning of the reign of the king they need.

And so it is a book about choosing a king. The people demand a king like everyone else has, and God gives them the king they have chosen— Saul. It is a disaster. Then God chooses a king unlike any other, and gives him to the people—David.

And in David, we see the ruler that God's people need. Courageous, godly, thoughtful, generous, patient. David is all those things—yet we also see his flaws. So David points us away from himself and to the ultimate ruler, the King God has chosen to rule his people eternally— David's descendant, Jesus.

For us today, as for Israel then, the challenge is: *Choose your king.* We must decide who will be king over our lives; who will have our ultimate allegiance. And 1 Samuel tells us not to look at outward appearance, but to look at the heart—to choose a ruler who gives, instead of takes. The message of 1 Samuel is: *Choose King Jesus.*

These six studies will take you through this tumultuous period of Israel's history. You'll read of battles and murders, women praying in anguish and men plotting in envy, shepherds and giants. You'll see the rise and fall of King Saul, and the rise and struggles of King David.

But more than any of that, you'll see Jesus Christ. And seeing him in and through 1 Samuel will enable you to see him with fresh colour and texture, and understand afresh what it means to follow him today; to choose the King whom God appointed—the King that God knows we need—to be King of our lives.

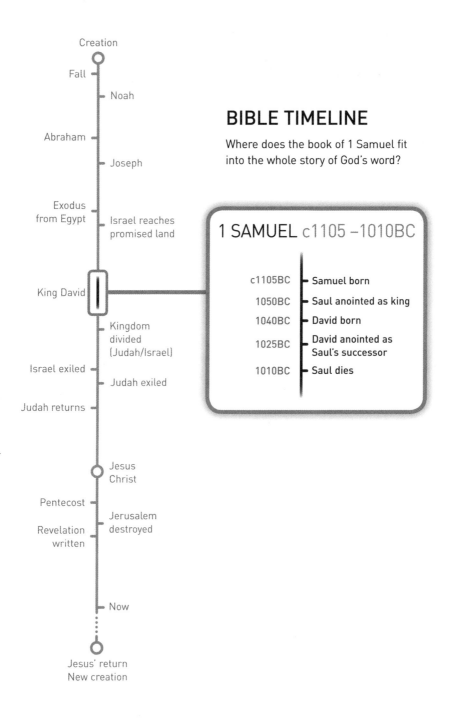

Creation

Fall

Noah

Abraham

Joseph

Exodus from Egypt

Israel reaches promised land

# BIBLE TIMELINE

Where does the book of 1 Samuel fit into the whole story of God's word?

King David

## 1 SAMUEL c1105 –1010BC

| c1105BC | Samuel born |
| 1050BC | Saul anointed as king |
| 1040BC | David born |
| 1025BC | David anointed as Saul's successor |
| 1010BC | Saul dies |

Kingdom divided (Judah/Israel)

Israel exiled

Judah exiled

Judah returns

Jesus Christ

Pentecost

Revelation written

Jerusalem destroyed

Now

Jesus' return
New creation

# 1

## 1 Samuel 1 – 3
# A TIME OF CRISIS

## ⊕ talkabout

1. How do you respond to feeling upset?

## ⊕ investigate

> ❯ Read 1 Samuel 1 v 1-20

2. How do verses 1-7 explain why Hannah is "weeping" and "downhearted" in verse 8?

Barrenness had added meaning in Old Testament Israel. God had promised that a child would be born who would save humanity; and Abraham had been promised that the child would come from his descendants, Israel (Genesis 3 v 15; Genesis 22 v 17-18). So infertility was a personal tragedy, as it is today, but it also carried a sense of exclusion from the purposes of God's people.

3. How does Hannah respond to her "deep anguish" (v 10) in verses 9-18?

**4.** Why does Hannah become pregnant (v 19-20)?

# → apply

**5.** What do these verses tell us about how we can and should respond when we are deeply upset about something in our lives?

• **Read Philippians 4 v 6-7.** How do we see Hannah living out this command in 1 Samuel 1?

# ↓ investigate

**▶ Read 1 Samuel 1 v 21 – 2 v 11**

Just as she promised (1 v 11), Hannah gives her son Samuel back to the Lord, to work in his service (v 24-28, 2 v 11). Between these verses, she prays, or sings, to God.

**6.** What does her song in 2 v 1-10 tell us about who God is and how he acts?

Hannah's song serves as the key to interpreting the story of 1 Samuel (and 2 Samuel). In these lines we hear all of the main themes of the book. The Lord humbles some and exalts others (v 7). It is not by strength that people prevail (v 9). God gives strength to his anointed king (v 10). And this last truth is remarkable, because at this point in the story there is no king in Israel! Hannah's prayer is saying: God's king is coming; and when he does, he will turn the world upside down.

**❯ Read 1 Samuel 2 v 12-36**

7. How are Eli's sons described (v 12)?

- What evidence does the writer give for this accusation (v 16-17)?

**DICTIONARY**

**Contempt (v 17):** total disrespect.
**Ephod (v 18):** the special tunic worn by a priest.
**Mediate/intercede (v 25):** speak up for someone else so that two enemies become friends.
**My dwelling (v 29):** the tabernacle.
**Disdained (v 30):** rejected.

- **Read Leviticus 7 v 31-32; 3 v 14-16.** How do these verses help us understand in what way Eli's sons' actions in 1 Samuel 2 v 13-16 were "treating the LORD's offering with contempt" (v 17)?

### ⊡ getting personal

The Bible tells us: "In view of God's mercy ... offer your bodies as a living sacrifice, holy and pleasing to God—this is your true and proper worship" (Romans 12 v 1). The sacrifice that belongs to the God who has saved us is our whole lives.

Is there any way in which you are acting like Eli's sons, and keeping what belongs to God for your own use?
This week, how will you offer God more completely what he deserves from you?

**8.** What does Eli do about this, and how effective is it (v 22-25)?

**9.** What does God say will happen to the house of Eli (v 27-36)?

(?) **explore more**

*optional*

▶ **Read 1 Samuel 4 v 1, 10-18**

*How does God's promise of judgment on the house of Eli come true? What does this remind us of, about God's word?*

In 2 v 29, God says that Eli has, along with his sons, fattened himself on the parts of the offerings that belonged to God, not to the priests. He has grown fat...

*How might this contribute to the way he dies in 4 v 18?*

Israel is in crisis. The priests were meant to point people to God, and offer sacrifices when people sinned against God. They were meant to "stand before the LORD to minister" (Deuteronomy 10 v 8). Instead, they are leading people away from God, and abusing the sacrificial system for their own ends. The proud, the arrogant and the full that Hannah sang about (1 Samuel 2 v 3-5) are found not among Israel's enemies, but among Israel's priests!

**10.** How do the descriptions of Samuel in chapter 2 give us some hope for Israel (v 11, 18, 21, 26)?

**▶ Read 1 Samuel 3 v 1 – 4 v 1**

This was a time when "the word of the LORD was rare" (v 1) and the people of God were in spiritual crisis.

11. What does God do about that in these verses?

## ⤳ apply

12. What does this tell us about what we most need when our lives, our church or our country is in crisis?

13. **Read Hebrews 1 v 1-2.** We have no Samuel today. But in what sense do we have a greater word-bringer than him?

## ▦ getting personal

If God's word is rare today, it is not because God is silent. He has spoken, loud and clear. If God's word is rare today, it is because people will not listen and Christians will not speak.

Are there any ways in which you are refusing to listen to God? How and where will you speak God's word in the coming week?

# ⊡ pray

**Thank God:**

- for prayer; that he hears and that he cares.
- for his word; that he speaks and that when he speaks, things change. Thank him most of all for revealing himself through his Son.

**Ask God:**

- to enable you to pray when you are feeling anguished or bitter.
- to entrust your greatest worries and disappointments to him and his sovereign purposes.
- to give you peace where you are feeling troubled. (If you are comfortable to, you could share prayer requests with the rest of the group.)

# 2 1 Samuel 8 – 10
# GIVE US A KING

*The story so far*

God answered Hannah's prayer and gave her a son, Samuel. Hannah dedicated Samuel to serving God, and God chose to speak through him to his people.

## ⊕ talkabout

1. What makes a good leader?

• Does that description change if the person is to lead a church (or group of churches)? How?

## ⊕ investigate

In chapters 4 – 6, there is war between Israel and the Philistines. After a series of desperate defeats, Israel learns to trust the LORD for victory, and the Philistines are defeated. With Eli and his sons dead, Samuel becomes both the priest and the judge (leader) of Israel (7 v 15-17).

Perhaps he is the leader God's people need—perhaps he is the king Hannah sang of (2 v 10)…

**▶ Read 1 Samuel 8 v 1-3**

DICTIONARY

**2.** What is the problem here?

Perverted (v 3):
made wrong.

**▶ Read 1 Samuel 8 v 4-22**

DICTIONARY

**3.** What do the people ask for, and why (v 4-5)?

Forsaking (v 8):
abandoning.
Vintage (v 15):
wine.

**4.** How does Samuel respond to this (v 6)?

• How does God respond to this (v 7-9)?

**5.** What does God, through Samuel, warn the people of, about the kind of king they are asking for (v 10-18)?

• How do the people respond (v 19-20)?

6. **Read Exodus 19 v 3-6; Deuteronomy 4 v 5-8.** What relationship was Israel meant to have with:

• God?

• the nations?

• So what does their request for a king like those of "all the other nations" mean they are saying about their identity?

⊡ **explore more**

*optional*

*What humans do in 1 Samuel 8 is what humans have done throughout history. How do we see the same decision being made in:*
• *Genesis 3 v 1-7*
• *John 19 v 1-16*
• *our own lives?*

## ⊡ apply

**7.** It is very easy for the church today to make the same mistake as Israel did back then. **Read 1 Peter 2 v 9** and then discuss these questions:

- We, like them, are to be a people whose behaviour is governed by God's ruling word. Are we? How is it tempting not to be?

- We, like them, are to be different, distinct and holy. Are we? How is it tempting not to be?

- We, like them, are supposed to be a light to the nations, declaring the praises of him who called us out of darkness into his wonderful light. Are we? How is it tempting not to be?

## ⊡ investigate

**⟩ Read 1 Samuel 9 v 1 – 10 v 1**

**8.** The Hebrew word "sa'al" means "asked for". So how is Saul a fitting name for Israel's first king?

> **DICTIONARY**
>
> **Benjaminite (9 v 1):** member of the tribe of Benjamin.
> **Anoint (v 16):** pour oil over someone's head to show they had been chosen for a particular role.
> **His inheritance (v 14):** Israel.

**❯ Read 1 Samuel 10 v 17-27**

9. What is encouraging about the beginning of Saul's kingship? What is concerning?

Samuel warned the people that a king of the kind they wanted would "take" (8 v 11); "take" (v 13); "take" (v 14); "take" (v 15); "take" (v 16); "take" (v 17).

10. How is King Jesus different?
    • Matthew 11 v 28

    • Mark 10 v 42-45

    • Luke 22 v 19

    • John 14 v 27

    • 2 Corinthians 8 v 9

    • Ephesians 4 v 11-12

## ⮕ apply

11. How should this affect our attitude towards Jesus, and his rule over us?

• How should this affect our expectations of what following God's King, rather than the kind of leader the world exalts, will be like?

## ⬆ pray

Choose some aspects of the character of Jesus Christ, and spend time praising him for who he is. Then go on to thank him for what he has given you.

Acknowledge (either aloud or, if you would rather, in silence) the ways in which you live with someone other than Jesus as your ruler. Thank God that his Christ came to offer you forgiveness for those ways.

Pray together for your church. Pray that your identity would be as God's people, and that you would not be shaped by the world's expectations or demands.

# 3 1 Samuel 11; 13; 15
# A GOOD START AND A HEAVY FALL

## The story so far

God answered Hannah's prayer and gave her a son, Samuel. Hannah dedicated Samuel to serving God, and God chose to speak through him to his people.

Israel rejected God and demanded a king like those of the other nations, despite being warned this king would exploit them. So God chose Saul to be that king.

## ⊕ talkabout

1. Why is it good to have "common sense"? Are there any times when it is good, or right, to ignore it?

## ⊕ investigate

> **Read 1 Samuel 11 v 1-11**

2. What is the problem (v 1-4)?

**DICTIONARY**

**Ammonite (v 1):** Ammon was a nation bordering Israel to the east.

3. How is Saul's response to the situation different to that of both the men of Jabesh Gilead and the people of Israel (v 5-11)?

• What does verse 6 suggest is the reason why Saul is able to do all this?

In 10 v 26-27, there was some doubt about whether Saul could be a king who saves Israel. Now Saul has shown that he is a king who can lead Israel into battle, and win. "So all the people … made Saul king in the presence of the LORD" (11 v 15). Saul's reign is recognised and established.

> **Read 1 Samuel 13 v 1-15**

**4.** Why, by verse 7, are Saul's troops either scattered or "quaking with fear"?

**5.** What does Saul do when Samuel does not turn up (v 8-10)?

• Why does he do this (v 11-12)?

**6.** What is Samuel's verdict on his actions (v 13-14)?

• How does verse 13 help us to understand why what he has done is so serious?

## ⮊ apply

Saul acted out of common sense instead of faith-filled obedience. He did not trust God to save his people, so he did not live in obedience to him. Instead, he took matters into his own hands.

**7.** How do we find this a temptation today? Why is it so tempting to live by sight, rather than by faith?

## ⊡ getting personal

Are there areas of your life in which...
• you are downplaying the seriousness of your sin?
• you are living by common sense rather than obedience to God?
How does this passage challenge you to change?
**Read 1 John 1 v 8 – 2 v 2**

## ⊡ explore more

> **Read 1 Samuel 13 v 23 – 14 v 15**

optional

Jonathan is Saul's son.

*What is Saul doing (v 2)? What does Jonathan do (v 1, 4-14)?*

In chapter 13, Saul uses his common sense instead of living by faith, and disobeys God.

*How does Jonathan give us a model of living by faith?*

## ⊡ investigate

> ❯ **Read 1 Samuel 15 v 1-3**

**8.** What does God, through Samuel, tell Saul to do as king of Israel?

This sounds alarmingly like ethnic cleansing. But in fact it is *ethical* cleansing—an act of judgment against sin. The Amalekites are to be punished "for what they did to Israel", attacking them as they escaped from Egypt (Exodus 17 v 8-16)—they did not die because they were Amalekites, but because they were sinners. Their destruction is a picture of what humanity deserves. When God's judgment comes, nothing is left.

> ❯ **Read 1 Samuel 15 v 4-9**

**9.** How well does Saul obey God's command?

> ❯ **Read 1 Samuel 15 v 10-35**

**10.** What is Samuel's verdict on Saul's obedience (v 17-19, 26-29)?

**DICTIONARY**

**Divination (v 23):** using occult to try to find out spiritual truths.
**Idolatry (v 23):** worshipping something other than God.
**Violated (v 24):** broken.

**11.** What excuses does Saul offer?

• v 15

• v 20

• v 21

• v 24

## ⊖ apply

**12.** What does God delight in (v 22)?

• What are the modern-day equivalents of "burnt offerings and sacrifices" that we can perform while failing truly to obey God?

**13.** How might we offer the kinds of excuses that Saul did?

## ⊞ getting personal

There are two unambiguous measures of faith: the pursuit of obedience, and real repentance when we fail to obey. God sees through our efforts to downplay or excuse our sin.

Is there anything you need to repent of, which you've been ignoring or excusing?

Remember, "he who is the Glory of Israel does not lie or change his mind" (v 29). This means he will judge those who are not repentant, as he has promised. But it also means that he will save those who do repent, as he has promised.

How does this encourage you to repent?

## ↥ pray

Use the two "getting personal" boxes to prompt your prayers of confession and repentance.

Thank God that it is true that "if we confess our sins, he is faithful and just and will forgive us our sins and purify us from all unrighteousness … we have an advocate with the Father—Jesus Christ, the Righteous One" (1 John 1 v 9; 2 v 1).

# 4 1 Samuel 16 – 17
# THE KING WE NEED

## The story so far

God answered Hannah's prayer and gave her a son, Samuel. Hannah dedicated Samuel to serving God, and God chose to speak through him to his people.

Israel rejected God and demanded a king like those of the other nations, despite being warned this king would exploit them. So God chose Saul to be that king.

Despite a successful start to his reign, King Saul later disobeyed God twice. As a result, God rejected Saul as king and promised to take the kingdom from him.

## ⊕ talkabout

1. Why do appearances matter? How can they be deceiving?

## ⊕ investigate

> Read 1 Samuel 15 v 34 – 16 v 1

2. How do these verses mark a fresh start in the history of Israel?

> DICTIONARY
>
> **Horn (16 v 1):** container for oil, which would be used to anoint the new king.

**3.** What is different about this new king (end of verse 1; see also 8 v 18)?

> ❯ **Read 1 Samuel 16 v 2-14**

**DICTIONARY**

**Consecrate (v 5):** wash and put on clean clothes so that you are ceremonially "clean".

**4.** How are Samuel's ideas about what makes a good king different from God's view?

**5.** How do verses 13-14 mark a crucial change in both David's and Saul's lives?

## explore more

optional

Everything about this is surprising. Samuel is sent to a nowhere town in Israel, to anoint a youngest son, a mere shepherd-boy. And the effects of this moment are still being felt in our world today.

> ❯ **Read 2 Samuel 7 v 11b-14; Micah 5 v 2-4; Isaiah 11 v 1-10**

*What does God promise about one of David's descendants in these verses?*

It's not surprising that the Gospel writers go to great lengths to show that Jesus is David's son, the ultimate Christ—the one born in Bethlehem and who brings all the blessings of Isaiah 11.

## ➔ apply

**6.** In what ways can we look at the outward appearance, rather than at the heart, when it comes to:

• religion?

• leadership?

## ⊡ getting personal

Samuel had to appoint a king. In a sense, it is a task we all have—we must choose who will be king over our lives. Who or what will have our ultimate allegiance?

What are the things or people who compete for rule over your heart?

**Read Matthew 11 v 28-29**

How is God's chosen King, Jesus Christ, a better ruler than those things? How will you joyfully submit to his rule?

## ⊡ investigate

**❯ Read 1 Samuel 17 v 1-58**

The story of David and Goliath is, of course, one of the most famous episodes in the entire Bible.

DICTIONARY

**Philistines (v 1):** long-time enemy of Israel.
**Greaves (v 6):** shin-armour.
**Uncircumcised (v 26):** ie: not part of God's people.

**7.** Why is David confident of victory when other Israelites—who are older, stronger and better-armed than him—refuse to face Goliath?

• v 32-37

• v 45-47

In verses 5-7, Goliath's armour is described in uncharacteristic detail. Verse 5 sums it up as (literally) "scales". The picture is not only of Goliath as a giant, but as a serpent, or snake.

**8.** **Read Genesis 3 v 1-7 and 13-15.** What is the significance of God's chosen king defeating the snake-like enemy?

• **Read 2 Samuel 7 v 11b-14.** Years after David defeats Goliath, God will promise him that he will have a descendant who is a greater king even than him. What can we look to that greater king to do for God's people?

# ⊟ apply

The good news of the Bible is not that we are called to be like David, facing our giants. It is that we have a David, who has faced our greatest enemies for us—the Lord Jesus, who has conquered the devil and defeated death. As we read the account of David and Goliath, we are not to put ourselves into David's shoes—that is Jesus' place. He is the anointed one—the Christ—who saves his people.

So, where *do* we find ourselves in the story?

**9.** How is it possible for us to be like:

• the Israelites (v 8-11)?

• Eliab (v 28)?

• Saul (v 33, 38-39)?

# ⊡ investigate

**10.** What is the role that God's people *do* play in the story (v 51-53)?

# ➔ apply

**11.** **Read 2 Corinthians 10 v 4-5 and Ephesians 6 v 10-17.** What does that look like for God's people today?

**12.** Why can we joyfully submit to the authority of Christ Jesus in our lives?

## ⊡ getting personal

Jesus has won the victory. He has defeated your greatest enemies. It is time to surge down the hillside and proclaim victory, to call those who once belonged to Satan to enjoy freedom under Christ's rule.

How will this change the way you view your life, and the way you speak to others, this week?

## ⬆ pray

Spend time praising God for all that Jesus has defeated for you, and all that he has triumphantly given you.

Speak to God about the various opportunities he gives you to tell others of Christ's victory. Pray for courage and the right words to be able to proclaim Christ. You might like to name individuals with whom you would particularly like to share the news of Jesus' victory this week.

# 5 1 Samuel 18; 24 – 26
# THE WILDERNESS YEARS

## The story so far

Israel rejected God and demanded a king like the other nations, despite being warned that this king would exploit them. So God chose Saul to be that king.

Despite a successful start to his reign, King Saul later disobeyed God twice. As a result, God rejected Saul as king and promised to take the kingdom from him.

Through Samuel, God chose the shepherd-boy David to be the next king. David rescued Israel by defeating Goliath, their apparently invincible enemy.

## ⊕ talkabout

1. What do you expect the rest of your life to be like? What difference will it make that you are a Christian?

## ⊕ investigate

> **Read 1 Samuel 18 v 1-16**

2. Who loves David? Who doesn't love David?

> **DICTIONARY**
>
> **Covenant (v 3):** agreement.
> **Prophesying (v 10):** here, any effect that comes from being influenced by a spirit.

**3.** What reasons are given for Saul's attitude towards David?

Saul's dislike turns more and more to murderous hatred. So he manoeuvres David into a position where his enemies may well defeat him (18 v 20-25). When this fails, he seeks to have him murdered (19 v 1, 9-12). He massacres some priests who give David shelter (22 v 17-19).

**4.** Read 1 Samuel 19 v 11-12; 21 v 1; 21 v 10 – 22 v 5; 23 v 15, 24-25. Plot David's escape routes on the map.

**5.** In chapter 16, God chose David as the next king of his people. In chapter 17, David defeated Israel's greatest enemy. Why is what happens to him next surprising?

⊡ **explore more**

optional

We have seen Saul's attitude towards David, driven by the knowledge that, if David lives, Saul's family will not rule (20 v 30-31).

**❯ Read 1 Samuel 18 v 1-4; 19 v 1-3; 20 v 12-17**

*Jonathan is Saul's son and heir. How is his attitude towards David different to his father's?*

*Why is his recognition of David as God's chosen king costly for him personally?*

Jonathan gives up the future of his house—yet in doing so, he gains its future under David's protection (20 v 15-17). **Read 2 Samuel 9 v 1-13.**

*Jonathan is often held up to us as a model of a good friend. But how is he, much more than this, the model of a good follower of God's King?*

⇥ **apply**

David experienced life on the margins, facing rejection. His greater descendant, Jesus, would too. Read Matthew 8 v 20; 13 v 53-57. And Jesus told his followers: "The student is not above the teacher, nor a servant above his master" (Matthew 10 v 24).

**6.** So what does David's experience tell us to expect our lives will be like as people chosen by God?

• What truth could David hang onto in these "wilderness years" (1 Samuel 23 v 16-17)?

**7.** When do we find it hardest to remember that the Christian life involves suffering before glory? What happens to our perspective of ourselves and of God when we forget this?

• What truths can we hang onto in wilderness times?

## getting personal

"We must go through many hardships to enter the kingdom of God" (Acts 14 v 22). In the Christian life, hardship is a must, not an option.

What are your expectations for your life as a Christian? Glory and comfort, or suffering and then glory?

Are there ways in which you need to re-set your expectations?

Are there any ways in which you are demanding that God take away some difficulty, instead of seeking to serve him during that difficulty?

## investigate

In chapters 24 – 26, David faces three trials. Each time, he is being tempted not to be the kind of king that God wants him to be.

**8.** Skim-read each chapter. What is David being tempted to do? What does he do instead?

• 24 v 1-22 (especially v 3-7, 10-13)

• 25 v 1-44 (especially v 21-34)

• 26 v 1-25 (especially v 7-11)

**9.** Imagine David had given in to each temptation. What kind of a king would he have been by the time he ruled over Israel?

**10.** **Read Luke 4 v 1-13.** What was Jesus, David's greater son, being tempted to do in the wilderness? What did he do instead?

• Imagine Jesus had given in to each temptation. What kind of a King would he be?

## ⮕ apply

**11.** What temptations do we face when life seems particularly difficult, or unfair, or to be going wrong?

• What do David and Jesus teach us about how to resist those temptations?

As we have seen, "we do not have a high priest who is unable to feel sympathy for our weaknesses, but we have one who has been tempted in every way, just as we are—yet he did not sin" (Hebrews 4 v 15).

**12.** How should this truth affect:

• your view of Jesus?

• your response to any struggles you are facing?

## ☺ getting personal

When you are in the wilderness, it is no more—it can never be more—than Jesus has experienced. Since he came through the wilderness, it is no more—it can never be more—than he can help you with, and help you through. And when you give into temptation, you can look to his faithfulness and know that his obedience has been given to you. You can approach a God who knows, understands, listens and helps.

Do you need to do this today?

## ⬆ pray

Thank Jesus that he is a King who has walked through the wilderness.

Speak to him now about ways in which you are suffering or struggling. Ask him to keep you obedient to him and trusting in him, like David.

# 6 1 Samuel 28; 30 – 31
# THE KING IS DEAD...

## The story so far

Despite a successful start to his reign, King Saul later disobeyed God twice. As a result, God rejected Saul as king and promised to take the kingdom from him.

Through Samuel, God chose the shepherd-boy David to be the next king. David rescued Israel by defeating Goliath, their apparently invincible enemy.

Saul, threatened by David's successes, tried to kill him. In fear of his life, David fled to the wilderness, but he refused to kill Saul when he had the chance.

## ⊕ talkabout

**1.** Why do people try to contact the dead?

## ⊥ investigate

By the beginning of chapter 28, Samuel is dead (25 v 1), and David is living among the Philistines, under the protection of one of their kings, Achish. But there is about to be war between Israel and the Philistines. David has placed himself in a difficult position—but not as difficult as the position Saul is about to put himself in.

> **DICTIONARY**
>
> **Mediums and spiritists (v 3):** people who claimed to be able to consult with the dead.
> **Urim (v 6):** a special object that was part of the way God guided his people (probably Saul didn't even have it at this stage, as it was sited in the ephod, which was with David, see 23 v 6).

**❯ Read 1 Samuel 28 v 1-25**

**2.** Why does Saul end up consulting a medium (v 5-7, 15)?

What exactly is going on when someone consults a medium to contact the dead? Many mediums are fakes, preying on vulnerable people (the woman at Endor may be one, which would explain her surprise when Samuel appears in 28 v 12).

But there is a spiritual world alongside the world we see—and there can be real encounters with it. But these encounters are not with departed loved ones, but with demons. The Bible is clear that the dead do not speak and they do not haunt this earth. God explicitly prohibits his people from visiting mediums and spirtiualists, "for you will be defiled by them" (Leviticus 19 v 31).

So what is happening at Endor? This is one of the few times in history when someone really does appear from the dead—not because of the abilities of the medium, but because God allows it to happen.

**3.** And what is the message Samuel brings to Saul (1 Samuel 28 v 16-19)?

**4.** **Read Isaiah 8 v 19.** What should God's people not do, and what should they do?

**5.** **Read Matthew 28 v 18-20; John 20 v 19, 26.** Where do we find the true presence of God and a real reassurance from God?

- How is what we hear from Jesus very different from what Saul heard from Samuel?

## ⮕ apply

Using a medium tends to be motivated by seeking the presence of someone beyond the grave; or seeking reassurance about life beyond the grave.

**6.** Why does knowing the Lord Jesus mean we do not need to do either?

- We might not use a medium; but how is it possible to seek a loving presence, or some reassurance, in places other than in God's Son?

## ⊡ getting personal

In Mark 9 v 7, as Jesus stand on the top of a mountain in all his heavenly glory, a voice from heaven tells those watching how to respond. It does not say: *Gaze at him*. It does say: "Listen to him".

We do not need to consult the dead. We do not need to wonder what God thinks. We do not need to worry about the future. We have Jesus.

How does this comfort you? How does it challenge you?
How well are you listening to him?

## ⬇ investigate

David is saved from his dilemma by the other Philistine kings. Because they do not trust this Israelite to fight his own people, Achish sends David and his men away from the battle, back to their base at Ziklag.

### ❯ Read 1 Samuel 30 v 1-31

**7.** What does David find in Ziklag (v 3-6)? How is this a crisis for his leadership?

## → apply

**8.** What does David's reaction teach us about how to respond to a crisis in a godly way?

• v 6b:

• v 7-8 (Hint: the ephod was part of the means God had given his people to find his wisdom):

## ⊎ investigate

**9.** When David pursues the Amalekites, what is the end result (v 17-20)?

**10.** What kind of king does David show himself to be in verses 21-31?

**❯ Read 1 Samuel 31 v 1-13**

**11.** Saul has been the architect of his own downfall throughout his reign. How is the manner of his death a fitting end for him?

The king is dead. And we know who the next king will be, because God has chosen him. In 2 Samuel 2 v 1-4, the tribe of Judah anoint David as their king; after a war with one of Saul's surviving sons, David emerges as king of all Israel (5 v 1-5). The stage is set for the reign of Israel's greatest Old Testament king, who in each stage of his life points us to the greatest King of all, the Lord Jesus Christ.

## ➡ apply

**12.** How has this history of Saul and David shown you:
- how you are tempted to choose the wrong kind of ruler?

- how great it is to live under the rule of God's chosen King?

- how to respond to difficulty as David did?

## ⬆ pray

Use your answers to Questions Six and Twelve to prompt you to praise God, confess to God, and ask God to help you live joyfully with Jesus as King.

# Choose
# your king
## LEADER'S GUIDE

# Leader's Guide

## INTRODUCTION

Leading a Bible study can be a bit like herding cats—everyone has a different idea of what the passage could be about, and a different line of enquiry that they want to pursue. But a good group leader is more than someone who just referees this kind of discussion. You will want to:

• correctly understand and handle the Bible passage. But also…

• encourage and train the people in your group to do this for themselves. Don't fall into the trap of spoon-feeding people by simply passing on the information in the Leader's Guide. Then…

• make sure that no Bible study is finished without everyone knowing how the passage is relevant for them. What changes do you all need to make in the light of the things you have been learning? And finally…

• encourage the group to turn all that has been learned and discussed into prayer.

Your Bible-study group is unique, and you are likely to know better than anyone the capabilities, backgrounds and circumstances of the people you are leading. That's why we've designed these guides with a number of optional features. If they're a quiet bunch, you might want to spend longer on *talkabout*. If your time is limited, you can choose to skip *explore more*, or get people to look at these questions at home. Can't get enough of Bible study? Well, some studies have optional extra homework projects. As leader, you can adapt and select the material to the needs of your particular group.

So what's in the Leader's Guide? The main thing that this Leader's Guide will help you to do is to understand the major teaching points in the passage you are studying, and how to apply them. As well as guidance on the questions, the Leader's Guide for each session contains the following important sections:

## THE BIG IDEA

One or two key sentences will give you the main point of the session. This is what you should be aiming to have fixed in people's minds as they leave the Bible study. And it's the point you need to head back toward when the discussion goes off at a tangent.

## SUMMARY

An overview of the passage, including plenty of useful historical background information.

## OPTIONAL EXTRA

Usually this is an introductory activity that ties in with the main theme of the Bible study, and is designed to "break the ice" at the beginning of a session. Or it may be a "homework project" that people can tackle during the week.

So let's take a look at the various different features of a Good Book Guide:

## ⊕ talkabout

Each session kicks off with a discussion question, based on the group's opinions or experiences. It's designed to get people talking and thinking in a general way about the main subject of the Bible study.

# ⬇ investigate

The first thing you and your group need to know is what the Bible passage is about, which is the purpose of these questions. But watch out—people may come up with answers based on their experiences or teaching they have heard in the past, without referring to the passage at all. It's amazing how often we can get through a Bible study without actually looking at the Bible! If you're stuck for an answer, the Leader's Guide contains guidance for questions. These are the answers to direct your group to. This information isn't meant to be read out to people—ideally, you want them to discover these answers from the Bible for themselves. Sometimes there are optional follow-up questions (see ✅ in guidance on questions) to help you help your group get to the answer.

# 🔅 explore more

These questions generally point people to other relevant parts of the Bible. They are useful for helping your group to see how the passage fits into the "big picture" of the whole Bible. These sections are OPTIONAL—only use them if you have time. Remember that it's better to finish in good time having really grasped one big thing from the passage, than to try and cram everything in.

# ➔ apply

We want to encourage you to spend more time working at application—too often, it is simply tacked on at the end. In the Good Book Guides, apply sections are mixed in with the investigate sections of the study. We hope that people will realize that application is not just an optional extra, but rather, the whole purpose of studying the

Bible. We do Bible study so that our lives can be changed by what we hear from God's word. If you skip the application, the Bible study hasn't achieved its purpose.

These questions draw out practical lessons that we can all learn from the Bible passage. You can review what has been learned so far, and think about practical differences that this should make in our churches and our lives. The group gets the opportunity to talk about what they personally have learned.

# 🙂 getting personal

These can be done at home, but it is well worth allowing a few moments of quiet reflection during the study for each person to think and pray about specific changes they need to make in their own lives. Why not have a time for reporting back at the beginning of the following session, so that everyone can be encouraged and challenged by one another to make application a priority?

# ⬆ pray

In Acts 4 v 25-30 the first Christians quoted Psalm 2 as they prayed in response to the persecution of the apostles by the Jewish religious leaders. Today however, it's not as common for Christians to base prayers on the truths of God's word as it once was. As a result, our prayers tend to be weak, superficial and self-centred rather than bold, visionary and God-centred.

The prayer section is based on what has been learned from the Bible passage. How different our prayer times would be if we were genuinely responding to what God has said to us through his word.

# 1
## 1 Samuel 1 – 3
# A TIME OF CRISIS

## THE BIG IDEA

As God's people, we can pray honestly, emotionally, and trustingly, and then be at peace. And as God's people, we need to listen to and trust in God's word as all we need.

## SUMMARY

The beginning of 1 Samuel is the story of Samuel's mother, Hannah. She is barren, and her husband's other wife is fruitful. Barrenness in Old Testament Israel was not only a personal tragedy; it also carried the sense of exclusion from the purposes of God's people, because God had promised to send a child who would reverse the effects of the fall (Genesis 3 v 15).

While others mocked or pitied Hannah, Hannah herself responded to her plight by praying. We see that prayer involves pouring out our souls to God (1 Samuel 1 v 15), bringing our anguish and needs to him, and trusting in God to care for us.

God grants Hannah's prayer for a son, and she gives birth to Samuel. This is what prompts her song of praise in 2 v 1-10, which sets out many of themes of the whole of 1 and 2 Samuel. The key verses are verse 2, that there is no one else like God; verse 7, that God raises up some and brings others down; and verse 10, where Hannah sings of how God will strengthen his king. This is strange, since at this point Israel has no king. Hannah's song is saying: *God's king is coming; and when he does, he will turn the world upside down.*

1 Samuel 2 continues by following Samuel to the house of God, where he "ministered

before the LORD" (2 v 11). The house of God is where the priests offer sacrifices for the people to God, but it has become horribly compromised. The high priest, Eli, is allowing his sons to steal both from the people and God by keeping the best parts of the sacrificed meat for themselves. This is a nation in spiritual crisis.

How does God respond? By speaking through Samuel (3 v 11-14, 19-21). God gives Samuel a word of judgment against Eli and his family; as the story unfolds, Samuel will also be the means by which God chooses the king to lead his people well. When there is a crisis, God sends his word. As his people, when we face difficulties either in our personal lives or more widely in society, what we most need is to listen to and pass on his word. But we do not have a Samuel figure today. We have a greater prophet—God's final revelation in the person of his Son, Jesus (Hebrews 1 v 1-2).

## OPTIONAL EXTRA

People's names and their meanings are very significant in 1 Samuel. Before the session, research what your group members' names mean (there are lots of websites that do this, though they often disagree with each other!). Prepare two separate lists and challenge your group to match the names with the meanings. Do your group members suit what their names mean? Remind your group of the activity when you reach Q4.

## GUIDANCE FOR QUESTIONS

**1. How do you respond to feeling upset?** There is no right way to respond (though there are some wrong ones!).

Let your group share their answers and experiences.

**2. How do verses 1-7 explain why Hannah is "weeping" and "downhearted" in verse 8?**
- v 2: She had no children, while Peninnah (her husband's other wife) did.
- v 5: She was unable to have children. Whatever the medical causes for Hannah's barrenness, ultimately it was God who had closed her womb.
- v 6: "Her rival [Peninnah] kept provoking her" each time they went up to Shiloh to worship God and make sacrifices to him.
- v 7: This went on for years.

**3. How does Hannah respond to her "deep anguish" (v 10) in verses 9-18?**
She weeps and she prays (v 10). She asks God to "remember me" (ie: act on her behalf) and give her a son (v 11), promising to give him back to God. She pours out her soul to God (v 15). She is so emotional as she prays that she seems drunk (v 13-14). After praying like this, "her face was no longer downcast".

**4. Why does Hannah become pregnant (v 19-20)?** Because, as Hannah and Elkanah made love, "the LORD remembered her" (v 19). God had closed her womb (v 5); God now opened it so that she could fall pregnant. Hannah herself knows why she finally has a son: because God heard her when she asked in prayer (v 20).
**Note:** The name "Samuel" actually means "his name is God", but the Hebrew word "ask for" is *sa'al*, which is close enough to "Samuel" for Hannah's comment in verse 20 to make sense.

**5. APPLY: What do these verses tell us about how we can and should respond**

**when we are deeply upset about something in our lives?** We are not to pretend we are OK. Hannah talks of her "misery" (v 11) and says she is "deeply troubled" (v 15).
But we are to pray. We know that God is sovereign over our suffering, and so he is able to help.
And we are to pour out our hearts in prayer. There is a brand of spirituality that says true prayer is about quiet and calm contemplation. But Hannah's prayer is anguished and emotional! If you are experiencing bitterness, then you are in a good palace to pray well. One of the reasons we do not pray more is that we do not feel the need to pray. When something happens that deeply upsets us, we realise that we need God. Great praying comes from a deep sense of our need and a deep sense of God's care.
Finally, we are to strive to be at peace, once we have prayed. In verse 18, Hannah eats and is no longer downcast. She does not yet know how God will answer her prayer—but the point is that she *has* prayed, and now she is happy to leave it with God. She knows God knows what is best and will do what is best, so she can be at peace. So can we.

- **Read Philippians 4 v 6-7. How do we see Hannah living out this command in 1 Samuel 1?** Hannah does not continue in her bitterness and sadness. She presents her requests to God. And then she knows the peace of God, which transcends all understanding.

**6. What does [Hannah's] song in 2 v 1-10 tell us about who God is and how he acts?**
- He delivers his people, rescuing them (v 1).
- He is unique, and uniquely pure (holy) (v 2).

- He knows what is really going on, and what people really think; and he weighs all our deeds in judgment (v 3).
- He humbles the strong and lifts the weak—he is a God who reverses things (v 4-8a).
- He is the Creator (v 8b).
- He looks after his people and judges his enemies (v 9).
- Human power does not count, because God is much more powerful (v 9b-10).
- He will judge (v 10).
- He will give strength and glory to his king ("his anointed" is another way of saying "his king") (v 10).

⊗

- **Read a song by another woman, Mary, who had a very unlikely son: Luke 1 v 46-55. What similarities do you see with Hannah's prayer-song?**
  - Both rejoice (v 47, 1 Samuel 2 v 1).
  - God is holy (v 49, 1 Samuel 2 v 2).
  - God opposes and humbles the proud, but lifts the humble (v 51-53, 1 Samuel 2 v 4-8).

One other similarity is less obvious: Hannah speaks of how God will give strength to his king (1 Samuel 2 v 10), a king who has not yet come, but for whom her son will prepare the way. Mary is singing because God's ultimate King is coming—he is growing in her womb.

**7. How are Eli's sons described (v 12)?**
Scoundrels—literally, "sons of wickedness".

- **What evidence does the writer give for this accusation (v 16-17)?**
  - The servants they sent threatened people bringing sacrifices (v 16).
  - They were treating sacrifices offered to God with contempt—a great sin (v 17).
- **Read Leviticus 7 v 31-32; 3 v 14-16.**

**How do these verses help us understand in what way Eli's sons' actions in 1 Samuel 2 v 13-16 were "treating the LORD's offering with contempt" (v 17)?**
- v 13-14: The priests were entitled to the breast and right thigh of the sacrifices that the people brought—the rest (apart from the parts reserved for God, see below) was eaten by those who brought the sacrifice. Hophni and Phinehas get their servant to take whatever meat he can spear with a fork. They are stealing the food being offered for sacrifice.
- v 15-16: The fat of the meat was God's "portion"—neither the priests nor the people were to eat it. But Hophni and Phinehas insisted on taking the meat with the fat still on, by force if necessary. They were robbing God.

**8. What does Eli do about this, and how effective is it (v 22-25)?** He hears what they are doing and confronts them. But they don't listen to him (v 25). (The end of verse 25 suggests that they are so sinful that God has already declared his verdict—they are so far gone into sin that they cannot turn back.)
**Note:** v 29 suggests that Eli is complicit in their sin; he is also fattening himself on the "choice parts" of the sacrifices that belong to God; and he cares more about his sons than about God. After all, he is the high priest and could end the employment in the tabernacle of his sons, but he does not.

**9. What does God say will happen to "the house of Eli" (v 27-36)?**
- They will be disdained (v 30).
- A time is coming when none of Eli's family will live to old age (v 31-32).
- Most (eventually all) of Eli's family will be stopped from "serving at my altar" (v 33).

God's judgment on this family who have so exploited their position as priests is that they will be removed from being priests.

**EXPLORE MORE**
**Read 1 Samuel 4 v 1, 10-18. How does God's promise of judgment on the house of Eli come true?** His sons are killed in battle. The shock is so great that Eli falls off his chair and dies. And the shock of all that is sufficient to send his daughter-in-law into labour, which she does not survive. (You could also turn to 1 Kings 2 v 26-27, where Eli's descendants are finally removed from the priesthood.)
**What does this remind us of, about God's word?** It comes true. What God says will happen, will happen. Here, it is judgment that is promised and that comes to pass. But of course, God also promises in his word to forgive and save those who turn back to him.
**How might this [Eli growing fat by eating the parts of the offering that belonged to God, 2 v 29] contribute to the way he dies in 4 v 18?** The fat of the sacrifice belonged to God, and had to be burned off. But Eli and his sons ate the fat, which fattened them (2 v 29). Eli had literally stolen what belonged to God and carried it round his waist. And so he was too heavy for his chair to support him well, and he fell off and died. Eli's sin brought him down and killed him.

**10. How do the descriptions of Samuel in chapter 2 give us some hope for Israel (v 11, 18, 21, 26)?** Samuel "ministered before the LORD". The verb "minister" is usually used to describe the activity of priests. So while Eli and his sons are busily corrupting the priesthood and facing God's judgment for doing so, Samuel is doing the job of a priest, as a replacement of the

failing house of Eli. It is a glimmer of hope.

**11. What does God do about that [spiritual crisis in Israel] in these verses?** He speaks to Samuel and shares his plans with him (v 11-14); and he speaks to Israel through Samuel as he reveals himself to Samuel through his word (v 19-21). God's response to crisis and compromise is to send his word, by raising up a prophet.

**12. APPLY: What does this tell us about what we most need when our lives, our church or our country is in crisis?** Very simply, we need God's word.

⊗

• **What does this mean in practice?** We need to be reading the Bible, engaging with the preaching of our church, speaking God's word to each other, and reminding our own hearts of God's word. We need to look to God's word for comfort and guidance, and trust that it is true and powerful. We don't need legislation, gimmicks or entertainment; we need God's powerful word for our lives and to share with others.

**13. APPLY: Read Hebrews 1 v 1-2. We have no Samuel today. But in what sense do we have a greater word-bringer than him?** Jesus is the word of God; the ultimate prophet. There is no greater revelation of God and his plans and purposes than his Son, who we see in the Scriptures that promise his coming (the Old Testament) and record his coming (the New Testament). So we shouldn't expect or demand that God speak to us as he spoke to Samuel, or that he should choose a Samuel for us to listen to. God has spoken to us in his Son. And we should listen.

# 2 1 Samuel 8 – 10
# GIVE US A KING

## THE BIG IDEA
God's people tend to look to the wrong ruler, for the wrong reasons; in Jesus, God has given us the King we need, rather than the one we naturally demand.

## SUMMARY
Just as Eli's sons were ungodly, so Samuel's do not "follow his ways" (8 v 3). So the elders of Israel ask Samuel to "appoint a king to lead us" (v 5).

God has promised his people a king to lead them (eg: Genesis 17 v 6, 16; Deuteronomy 17 v 14-20). Hannah had spoken of his coming king (1 Samuel 2 v 10). But this request for a king is met by God's disapproval: "They have rejected me" (8 v 7). Why? Because the people are asking for the wrong king with the wrong motives. They want a king "such as all the other nations have" (v 5). They don't want the king God has promised. They want a king like everyone else has. They want Israel to be like all the surrounding nations. This is a rejection of their identity as God's holy, chosen, distinctive people. It is a rejection of God and their relationship with him.

Through Samuel, God warns them what the king they want will be like—he will take, take, take (v 10-17). They will regret being under his rule (v 18). But the people are insistent. So God gives them the kind of king they demand, a man named Saul (chapter 9). Yet he is lost before he is even acclaimed as ruler (10 v 20-23). Nevertheless, he is both chosen by God and recognised by most of the people (v 24), and verse 25 suggests that he will be guided by God's law and God's prophet. Just possibly, Saul will turn out to be the king God's people need, rather than merely the king they want.

Ultimately, though, the only man who is the King that people need is the Lord Jesus. His rule involves giving instead of taking. Q10 focuses on just how much Jesus gives to us as his people. We must all be ruled by someone, or something. That something will enslave us and take from us, unless it is the ruler who obeys God and leads us into obedience to God (and, indeed, gives us his obedience when and where we fail). If we expect Jesus to be a king like "the other nations have", he will disappoint us. If we want him to lead us into obeying God as his people, he will delight us.

## OPTIONAL EXTRA
Play a game where your members have to match the country to the leader. You could print the names of nations on slips of paper, and the names of their leaders on other slips, and ask the group (or pairs, "competing" against each other) to match them up. If you have time, you could print photos of the leaders, too.

As an extension, you could ask groups to guess which of the nations chose that leader, and which have had the leader chosen for them (eg: North Korea).

## GUIDANCE FOR QUESTIONS
**1. What makes a good leader?**
- **Does that description change if the person is to lead a church (or group of churches)? How?**

To keep the discussion brief, you could ask your group for one-word descriptions of a good leader. Make sure you answer the first part of the question before moving on to the second—the answers may differ. You could return to this discussion after Q5 (a description of how rulers usually lead) and Q10 (where you will look at the kind of King that Jesus is).

**2. What is the problem here [in 8 v 1-3]?** Samuel appoints his sons as leaders to follow him, but "his sons did not follow his ways" (v 3)—they are corrupt. The story of Eli is being repeated, and there are also echoes of Judges, where in the only previous episode of a son succeeding a father as ruler, Abimeleck led Israel after Gideon, and took the people into civil war.

**3. What do the people ask for, and why (v 4-5)?** "A king to lead us." Why?
(1) Samuel is old, and so the succession is important.
(2) His sons are not good heirs.
(3) "All the other nations" have a king.
At this stage in Israel's history, we would be expecting God to initiate the introduction of a king. A king has long been anticipated (eg: Genesis 17:6, 16) and the problem in the book of Judges was that "Israel had no king" (Judges 18 v 1; 21 v 25). Instead, the introduction of a king comes as a request from the elders.

• **Do you sympathise with them?** Perhaps we should. Israel at this point in their history was a loose confederation of tribes, with no standing army or central state structures. The central shrine at Shiloh is a disgrace (see last study). And they are facing the Philistines—a well-organised, aggressive alliance of powerful city-states. And each of those cities has a king… Added to this, the only man who has the status and the character to be able

to lead them is Samuel, and he is growing old. In this context, "a king to lead us and to go out before us and fight our battles" (v 20) sounds very sensible.

**4. How does Samuel respond to this (v 6)?** He is displeased.

• **Do you sympathise with him?** Perhaps we should—he has served Israel for decades, and now this is a criticism of his succession planning and a rejection of his sons (as well as a reminder that he is old!)

• **How does God respond to this (v 7-9)?** He tells Samuel that in fact this is a rejection of him, God, rather than of Samuel (v 7). He says it fits the Israelites' pattern of "forsaking" or abandoning him (v 8). And he tells Samuel to warn the people of what the king they want will do (v 9).

**5. What does God, through Samuel, warn the people of about the kind of king they are asking for (v 10-18)?** He will take:
• their sons as soldiers (v 11-12).
• their daughters as servants (v 13).
• their best fields as gifts for his favourites (v 14).
• a tenth of their crops and flocks (v 15, v 17a).
• their servants, cattle and donkeys for his own use (v 16).
• their own freedom (v 17b).
This king will be the kind of leader from whom the people find themselves crying out for a rescue (v 18).

• **How do the people respond (v 19-20)?** They insist they want a king over them, just like all the other nations have, to lead them into battle and fight for them.

**6. Read Exodus 19 v 3-6; Deuteronomy 4 v 5-8. What relationship was Israel meant to have with:**
• **God?** They were to be:
  • his "treasured possession" (Ex. 19 v 5).
  • "a kingdom of priests" (v 6—priests had particular access to God).
  • "a holy nation"—holy means pure and set apart; they were to be set apart for God, different to every other nation.
  • obedient to him (v 5; Deut 4 v 5-6).
• **the nations?** "A kingdom of priests" (v 6): priests represented God to people, so the nation of Israel was meant to show the world what God is like.
  Obeying God's law was meant to prompt surrounding nations to see that a nation under God's rule is wise and understanding (Deut. 4 v 6) and that there is no God like Israel's God (the Lord, v 7). In summary, Israel had a missional identity; they were meant to be like God so that they would reveal God to the nations.
• **So what does their request for a king like those of "all the other nations" mean they are saying about their identity?** By wanting to be just like all the other nations, they are rejecting their identity as God's people. Instead of being like God, they want to be like the nations. Instead of being ruled by God, they are following the ways of the nations. Instead of showing God to the nations, they want to be indistinguishable from the nations. And instead of trusting God to protect them, they want a king to do that.

**EXPLORE MORE**
**What humans do in 1 Samuel 8 is what humans have done throughout history.**

**How do we see the same decision being made in:**
• **Genesis 3 v 1-7?** Instead of listening to God and trusting his word, the first man and woman listen to the snake (ie: the devil) and trust him instead. They decide that they know better than God.

• **John 19 v 1-16?**
  • v 2-3: Instead of treating God's Son Jesus as King, the soldiers mock his claims.
  • v 12: The Jewish leaders (the descendants of Israel) are so determined not to have Jesus as their King that they pledge allegiance to a king who is not just like a king of the nations, but who is a king of the nations—the Roman occupier, Caesar.

• **our own lives?** In essence, whenever we sin, and particularly when we sin because others are doing so, we are choosing not to be like God or to reveal God or be ruled by him—just as happened in 1 Samuel 8.

**7. APPLY: It is very easy for the church today to make the same mistake as Israel did back then. Read 1 Peter 2 v 9 and then discuss these questions:** 1 Peter 2 v 9 uses the language of Israel's identity to describe the identity of the church. The church are the inheritors of Israel's status as God's special people, living like God to reveal God to those round us. So we are tempted in the same ways as Israel was back in 1 Samuel 8. For each of the parts to this question, ensure the discussion focuses on how your group and/or your church succeeds and fails to live as God's people (rather than on how other people or other churches fail). Your answers will vary depending on your context and culture.

• **We, like them, are to be a people whose behaviour is governed by God's ruling word. Are we? How is it**

tempting not to be?
- **We, like them, are to be different, distinct and holy. Are we? How is it tempting not to be?**
- **We, like them, are supposed to be a light to the nations, declaring the praises of him who called us out of darkness into his wonderful light. Are we? How is it tempting not to be?**

**8. [In 1 Samuel 9 v 1 – 10 v 1] The Hebrew word "sa'al" means "asked for". So how is Saul a fitting name for Israel's first king?** Through Samuel, God chooses Saul to be the first king (9 v 15-17; 10 v 1). He is, quite literally, the king the people have asked for—have "sa'al"ed—despite God's warnings about what he will be like. The king's name is a constant reminder that the people have been given what they asked for.

**9. [In 10 v 17-27] What is encouraging about the beginning of Saul's kingship? What is concerning?** Encouragingly, he is acclaimed by the people, as well as chosen by God (v 24). The rights and duties of the king are written down as a yardstick to judge Saul by (as God had commanded in Deuteronomy 17 v 14-20).
But there are concerns straight away. First, Saul is lost even before he begins to rule (v 21)—the man who is going to lead Israel into battle is hiding (v 22). The people will not trust God to deliver them (v 19), but they cannot even find their own king without God's help (v 22)! And not everyone believes that Saul is the man for the job (v 27), despite his selection by God.

**10. How is King Jesus different [to a king who takes, takes, takes]?** If you are short of time, split the group into pairs and take one or two of the verses each.
- **Matthew 11 v 28:** He gives rest (eternal

life, and the assurance of not needing to earn that life) to all who come to him.
- **Mark 10 v 42-45:** Jesus does not "lord it over" his people, but instead came to serve, to give his life to free his people.
- **Luke 22 v 19:** He gave his body to be broken on the cross so that his people could be forgiven.
- **John 14 v 27:** He gives peace with God to his people.
- **2 Corinthians 8 v 9:** He gave up the riches of heaven and became a poor man, condemned as a criminal, so that he could give his people eternal riches.
- **Ephesians 4 v 11-12:** He gives gifts to individuals among the church so that they can serve his people.

**11. APPLY: How should this affect our attitude towards Jesus, and his rule over us?** We can be joyful that we have a King who rules us in this way! It is easy for Christians to think of Jesus' rule as a burden or a drawback. But we will all have a ruler—it will be one we choose, or it will be the man God has chosen for us. Every other ruler (a person or a thing) will take from us; Jesus gives to us. So living under his rule can be and should be a joy. Obeying his commands, even when they make our life more difficult or mean we seem to miss out, is not just about gritting our teeth; we can do so with a smile, because he is the King who gives to his people.

- **How should this affect our expectations of what following God's King, rather than the kind of leader the world exalts, will be like?** It will mean us being different, and therefore misunderstood; and it will require us to be willing to serve and give, rather than be in it for ourselves.

# 3 1 Samuel 11; 13; 15
# A GOOD START AND A HEAVY FALL

## THE BIG IDEA
Sin is serious, and has serious consequences; and disobedience cannot be excused. But God delights in his people's obedience.

## SUMMARY
The passages included in this session start at the beginning of Saul's reign, and it's a hopeful start. Then they continue to his disobedience, which causes God to declare that the kingdom will be taken away from him.

In 11 v 1-15, we see Saul being used and exalted by God. Filled with the Spirit, Saul rescues God's people in Jabesh Gilead from Israel's enemies. At a moment when there seems to be no hope, God's king steps in to save. It is a good start to Saul's rule.

But in chapter 13, Saul goes wrong. His mistake is to disobey God by making a sacrifice, which is not his role to make. He does not keep the LORD's command because he does not trust the LORD to act. Instead, he takes matters into his own hands. He uses what we might call common sense instead of living in obedience to God. As a result, Samuel tells him that the kingdom will be taken from his family.

In chapter 15, we find Saul once again failing to obey God. This time, when he is told to destroy the Amalekites as a judgment on them for seeking to destroy Israel during the exodus, Saul obeys only partially. Despite offering a number of excuses, Samuel (and, more importantly, God) is not fooled. Disobedience is sin, and it is serious; again,

Samuel tells Saul that God has rejected his kingship because Saul has rejected God's rule (v 26).

It is easy to sympathise with Saul in chapters 13 and 15. But what matters is not what he succeeds in doing, but in what he fails to do, and why. He is disobedient to God because he thinks he knows better than God, and does not trust God to act for his people. And the narrative shows how seriously God takes disobedience, as well as reminding us that God delights in faithful obedience more than "religious" acts or rituals (v 22).

In the midst of this section, in 14 v 1-15, Saul's own son, Jonathan, provides a contrast to Saul's failings (see the Explore More in this study). Saul acts out of fear. But Jonathan acts in confident faith, trusting that God is sovereign and that he can save.

## OPTIONAL EXTRA
Play a game of "Consequences" (you can find instructions online if you type "how to play consequences" into Google). Point out that the hilarity of the game lies in the disconnect between each stage—the consequence doesn't fit the previous event. The world often thinks of sin in this way— we think it has no consequences, we don't spot its consequences in our lives, and we ignore the long-term effect it has on our eternity. We need passages such as this one to remind us that sin matters.

## GUIDANCE FOR QUESTIONS
**1. Why is it good to have "common sense"? Are there any times when**

**it is good, or right, to ignore it?** This discussion aims to pick up on both the way we can exalt what looks like common sense over obedience to God (when God's word "isn't realistic" or "just doesn't really work"), as we see Saul doing in Q4-5 and 7; and on the way we excuse our sin, as we see Saul doing in Q11.

Do tell your group members that they are not being judged on what they say in answer to this question! There is often a gap between what we know is true (that disobeying God's word is always serious) and how we think and live—this question is designed to help you discuss how you actually live in practice. You might like to start the discussion with a couple of ways in which you sometimes find yourself thinking that disobedience is justifiable or does not matter much.

**2. What is the problem (v 1-4)?** An Israelite town, Jabesh Gilead, is besieged by the king of the Ammonites, Nahash. He will let them make peace with him only if they agree to having one eye each gouged out. He wants to "bring disgrace on all Israel" (v 2). The leaders of Jabesh ask for seven days to see if anyone in the rest of Israel will come to their aid (v 3)—but the people merely "wept aloud", as though the situation was hopeless (v 4).

**3. How is Saul's response to the situation different both to that of the men of Jabesh Gilead and the people of Israel (v 5-11)?** The men of Jabesh Gilead want to be at peace with Nahash, even if it means submitting to him as their ruler (v 1). The men of Israel simply weep about the inevitable fate of the town (v 4). Saul is angry about the situation (v 6), summons Israel to fight (v 7-8), promises to rescue the town (v 9), and fights and defeats the

Ammonite besiegers (v 11).

• **What does verse 6 suggest is the reason why Saul is able to do all this?** "The Spirit of God came powerfully upon him." It is God who enables the ruler of his people to rescue them (see also Judges 3 v 10; 6 v 34; 15 v 14).

**4. Why, by verse 7, are Saul's troops either scattered or "quaking with fear"?** Because they are faced by a vast, well-equipped Philistine army.

**5. What does Saul do when Samuel does not turn up (v 8-10)?** It seems Saul has some arrangement with Samuel, that he will come to offer a sacrifice and bless the army. But as more and more troops desert, and Samuel does not show up, Saul offers the sacrifice himself (v 9)—at which point, Samuel arrives (v 10).

• **Why does he do this (v 11-12)?** Because, Saul says, the men are scattering; Samuel had not come as planned; and the Philistines were assembling to fight. He was about to fight, and the sacrifice had not been made; so he "felt compelled" to offer it himself.

**6. What is Samuel's verdict on his actions (v 13-14)?** "You have done a foolish thing." In the Old Testament, to live foolishly is to live as though God does not exist or does not matter (see Psalm 14 v 1). And so now, Saul's "kingdom will not endure".

• **How does verse 13 help us to understand why what he has done is so serious?** Samuel says: "You have not kept the command the LORD your God gave you". He did not trust that his role was to obey God, and that God's was to "[establish Saul's] kingdom over Israel".

Saul's problem is that he acted as though God would not act. He did not trust God to keep his promises.

**7. APPLY: How do we find this [acting based on common sense rather than obedience to God's word] a temptation today? Why is it so tempting to live by sight, rather than by faith?** You could think about the following areas:
- finances
- career (promotion, completing projects, cutting corners, etc)
- education (ours, or our family's)
- talking to non-Christians about Jesus
Living by sight is much easier than living by faith! It is how the world around us lives, and it does not require us to trust God.

**EXPLORE MORE**
**What is Saul doing (14 v 2)?** "Staying on the outskirts of Gibeah." The Philistines are overrunning his kingdom; but Saul is staying where he is, not fighting.
**What does Jonathan do (v 1, 4-14)?** He decides to "go over" to where the enemy is (v 1). And, despite being outnumbered, he knows that God may "act on our behalf" (v 6), seeks and finds confirmation that God will (v 8-12), trusts God (v 12), attacks, and scatters the Philistine detachment (v 13-14).
**How does Jonathan give us a model of living by faith?** He knows that God is sovereign, and will save if he chooses (v 6). And with confidence that God is on his side, he advances despite the numerical disadvantage. He knows that God's purposes are for his people to triumph over his people's enemies, and so he is brave in advancing. His trust in God leads him to take risks and override "common sense" in order to be part of God's plans.

**8. [In 15 v 1-3] What does God, through**

Samuel, tell Saul to do as king of Israel? To attack and completely destroy the Amalekites and all that belongs to them: men, women, children and animals.

- **What reason does God give for this command?** Verse 2: This destruction will be God's punishment on the Amalekites for their mistreatment of the Israelites when they first escaped from Egypt. If you have time, read Exodus 17 v 8-16.

**9. How well does Saul obey God's command?** He musters his troops (v 4), sets his ambush (v 5), isolates the Amalekites (v 6), attacks them (v 7), and "totally destroyed" them (v 8). In all this, he is obedient to God's command.
"But" Saul spares King Agag and "the best of" the animals (v 9). This goes against God's command, which was to "put to death" everything (v 3).

**10. What is Samuel's verdict on Saul's obedience (v 17-19, 26-29)?**
*Verses 17-19:* Samuel reminds Saul of God's favour to him (v 17) and the specifics of the command (v 18). So Saul's actions have not been in obedience (v 19). He took plunder for himself instead of doing what God wanted—so he has done "evil in the eyes of the Lord".
*Verses 26-29:* Saul has "rejected the word of the Lord" (v 26)—and so the verdict is that "the Lord has rejected you as king over Israel!" Saul's sin has serious consequences. This is pictured in the tearing of Samuel's robe (v 27-28)—Saul's kingdom will be torn away from him, because he has disobeyed the God who gave it to him. God is utterly consistent (v 29)—and he consistently judges and punishes sin.

**11. What excuses does Saul offer?**

- **v 15:** *Everyone else does it* (or: *It was someone else's fault*): Saul talks about what "The soldiers" did.

- **v 20:** *I did most of what you asked.* Saul says that he has spared Agag, but he did obey in destroying everything else. He uses obedience in some areas to try to excuse disobedience in another area.

- **v 21:** *My disobedience was for a godly reason.* Saul says that the best animals were not destroyed so that they could be sacrificed to God. His excuse is that his motives for his sin were good ones.

- **v 24:** "I was afraid of the men and so I gave in to them." Perhaps Saul really was worried about what others thought, or would do, and so gave in to pressure. Or perhaps he was casting round for another excuse (after all, he was the king over these people).

**12. APPLY: What does God delight in (v 22)?** Obedience. He delights in his people humbly obeying him because they trust him far more than he delights in people performing religious duties/rituals. Anyone can go through the religious motions, but to obey radically and riskily because we trust God is much harder. So what clearly shows our faith is the pursuit of obedience (Romans 1 v 5).

- **What are the modern-day equivalents of "burnt offerings and sacrifices" that we can perform while failing truly to obey God?** These vary from person to person and culture to culture, but include things like church attendance, Bible reading, street evangelism, volunteering on a church rota, and so on. Notice that none of these things are bad—in fact, all are good. But they can be used to mask and excuse disobedience in areas where we find living God's way costly or risky. And it is obedience that God delights in.

**13. APPLY: How might we offer the kinds of excuses that Saul did?** Go back through your answers to Q11 and think about what kinds of sins we offer those excuses for. You might like to think about sins such as law-breaking (eg: speeding); gossip; failing to answer someone's question about Christ; anger; etc.

# 4 1 Samuel 16 – 17
# THE KING WE NEED

## THE BIG IDEA

It is wonderful to live under the rule of God's chosen, rescuing king—even if the world does not think much of him.

## SUMMARY

Saul was the king Israel asked for; but he was not the king they needed. In chapters 13 – 15, he failed badly three times. In chapter 16, we are introduced to the king God's people need, but do not ask for. This is the king God chooses to rule them. He is not the king Samuel would choose, because the LORD does not look at appearances, but at the heart (16 v 7). He is David, a young shepherd-boy.

This shepherd boy will become Israel's greatest Old Testament king, or "christ". *Christos* is the Greek for "anointed one". Old Testament kings of Israel were not crowned with a crown, but were anointed with oil (the Hebrew for "anointed one" is "messiah"). And David will be the ancestor of the greatest King of all—Jesus. He, too, did not look like a king to the world—but God cares about the heart.

Chapter 17 takes us to one of the most famous stories in the whole Bible—David and Goliath. This study does not focus on the familiar narrative of the story, but rather looks at David's confidence in God to give him victory; the way Goliath is presented as a serpent, or snake, whom David defeats on behalf of God's powerless people; and God's people's role in enjoying the victory David has won for them by plundering the enemy's camp. Again David is a picture of a greater Christ who defeats the ultimate snake, the devil, and whose people enjoy that victory by plundering the devil's "camp" as we proclaim Jesus' rescue and rule.

## OPTIONAL EXTRA

Watch the clip from Episode Four of *The Bible* series which shows David defeating Goliath. (It takes some poetic license—David speaks some words from Psalm 23 as he advances towards Goliath.) At time of publication, you can find the clip at: http://bit.ly/1kCdEWo.

## GUIDANCE FOR QUESTIONS

**1. Why do appearances matter? How can they be deceiving?** You don't need to look for a definitive answer here. Most of us know that appearances don't/shouldn't matter, or that they should matter less; yet most of us still care about our own appearance more than we need to, and

judge others based on theirs. Of course, sometimes appearance is a good guide to what lies underneath; but at other times, it can be completely misleading. For every person who falls in love at first sight and continues with those feelings, there is someone who falls in love at first sight, and out of love on closer acquaintance!

**2. How do these verses [15 v 34 – 16 v 1] mark a fresh start in the history of Israel?** Saul has failed badly, and so God regrets making him king (15 v 35). But now there is an end to the time of mourning/regretting the way Saul is ruling. God tells Samuel to anoint a new king, whom God has chosen. There is a new beginning; Saul has been rejected, and a new king is coming.

**3. What is different about this new king (end of verse 1; see also 8 v 18)?** Though God did choose Saul, he was giving the people the king who they wanted. 8 v 18 makes clear that Saul was the king the people chose. Now, without the people doing anything at all, God tells Samuel that: "I have chosen one of [Jesse's] sons to be king" (16 v 1). This next king will be the king God gives his people, a man of his choosing.

**4. How are Samuel's ideas about what makes a good king different from God's view?** Samuel is impressed by Eliab (v 6), and thinks this must be the man God has chosen. Verse 7 shows that Samuel is struck by his appearance and his height. Eliab is Jesse's eldest, tallest son—kingly material. But "the LORD looks at the heart" (v 7). This is the key verse. God does not base his decisions on (and is not impressed by) outward appearances, but on heart realities. Jesse had not even thought to have his youngest son line up with the others, but had left him looking after the sheep (v 11). Yet this son, David, was the one God had chosen (v 12). It is reasonable to conclude that a shepherd boy cannot be king—but God does not operate by human reason.

**5. How do verses 13-14 mark a crucial change in both David's and Saul's lives?** David began the day as a youngest brother, a mere shepherd boy. He is now the anointed future king of Israel, filled with God's Spirit. Saul, on the other hand, is the rejected king, and the Spirit has "departed" from him.

The anointing of kings with oil was symbolic of an anointing with the Spirit of God, who in the Old Testament came upon people to equip them for specific tasks. So now David is given the authority and ability to rule God's people; Saul's authority and ability is removed.

**Note:** Someone may ask whether this means the removal of Saul's salvation. The answer is no—it is the removal of his ability to rule as God's authoritative king. Whether Saul was a true (but troubled) believer is hard to discern, though 10 v 9 does say that: "God changed Saul's heart".

**EXPLORE MORE**
**Read 2 Samuel 7 v 11b-14; Micah 5 v 2-4; Isaiah 11 v 1-10. What does God promise about one of David's descendants in these verses?**
*2 Samuel 7 v 11b-14:* Beyond David's own life, he will have "offspring" whose kingdom God will establish; who will build a house (temple) for God; whose throne will continue for ever; and who will enjoy a particularly close relationship with God. Intriguingly, though he will be punished (v 14), God's love will never be removed from him (v 15). David is a great christ; his descendant will be still greater.

*Micah 5 v 2-4:* Bethlehem, though a small town, will be the place from where a new ruler over Israel will come. Like David, he will be a "shepherd" (v 4), and he will bring security to Israel, and to "the ends of the earth".

*Isaiah 11 v 1-10:* A shoot from the stump of Jesse (we might say, someone in the family tree of Jesse) will be Spirit-filled, as David was (v 2); will fear the LORD and rule well, not judging based on appearances but on truth (v 3-5); and he will usher in a time of peace (v 6-9), drawing people from the nations to his banner (v 10).

**6. APPLY: In what ways can we look at the outward appearance, rather than at the heart, when it comes to:**
• **religion?** Any time we base our view of our (or someone else's) religion or acceptance before God on what we are doing, or not doing, or how others think of us, we are making the mistake of looking at outward appearance. It is very easy to do this: to assume we are saved people because of our church attendance, or baptism, or role within church, or deeds among the community, and so on; or because other people think of us as strong Christians. None of these are bad; but God looks at the attitudes of the heart.

• **leadership?** Both within and without the church, we find it easy to be swayed by how someone looks, how they dress, what others think of them, their sense of humour, etc. Again, none of these are bad things. But God looks at the attitudes of the heart. You might like to turn to Titus 1 v 6-9 to see what God looks for in leaders of his people.

**7. Why is David confident of victory when other Israelites—who are older, stronger and better-armed than him—**

**refuse to face Goliath?**

- **v 32-37:** Answering Saul's point that David is both too young and too inexperienced (v 33), David points out that, as a shepherd, he has risked his life to protect his flock. And he knows that it was God who protected him as he did so (v 37)—and that God will give him victory over "this uncircumcised Philistine" (v 36). David uses the word "uncircumcised" as a way of underlining the fact that Goliath is an enemy of God's people. Notice that David is willing to act as the shepherd of God's people, which is the role of the king, but a role that Saul will not fulfil. David is the good shepherd-king.

- **v 45-47:** He is facing Goliath armed not with weapons but in "the name of the Lord Almighty … whom you have defied" (v 45). David trusts God to give him victory, not his own strength (v 46-47—notice the echo of Hannah's song in 2 v 9-10). David is not basing his confidence on how mighty he is, nor being fearful because of how mighty Goliath is; he simply remembers how all-mighty God is.

**8. Read Genesis 3 v 1-7 and 13-15. What is the significance of God's chosen king defeating the snake-like enemy?** Goliath is presented to us as a serpent, or snake, covered in scales. Like Satan in Eden, Goliath is defying God's people and wielding the power of death. But God had promised that there would be enmity between Eve's offspring and the snake, and that one of her offspring would crush his head. Here, David defeats Goliath with a head wound. He defeats the snake-like man and his power over God's people, on behalf of God's people, none of whom were able to fight. So David is able to protect God's people by defeating the "snake"—he is suited to be Israel's king.

- **God told Samuel that he should not judge on appearances. How does the fight between David and Goliath underline this truth?** This is a fight between a badly-armed shepherd boy and an armoured, sword-wielding giant. Appearances suggest there can only be one winner. But the tallest man in history is brought low. The lesson that we should not judge by appearance applies not only to our choices, but also to our enemies.

- **Read 2 Samuel 7 v 11b-14. Years after David defeats Goliath, God will promise him that he will have a descendant who is a greater king even than him. What can we look to that greater king to do for God's people?** (If you did the Explore More section earlier, you will have already looked at these verses.)
David provides a picture of the ultimate King of God's people, his greater descendant, Christ Jesus. Jesus also faced a serpent—the devil himself—and defeated him through resisting his temptations and then dying on the cross for God's people, destroying the devil's power over us.
David represents the people in facing their enemy. His victory is their victory (just as his defeat would have been their defeat). So with Jesus; all that he wins, we enjoy as his people. Our future depends on his victory.
What we see in the Valley of Elah is a miniature version of the victory of Jesus.

**9. APPLY: How is it possible for us to be like:**
- **the Israelites (v 8-11)?** They are "dismayed and terrified" (v 11), because they know they cannot hope to defeat

Goliath. We can often live as though Jesus has not triumphed over death, and is not ruling over life—so we despair about things, or grow anxious about the future. We are right to realise that we cannot rely on our own abilities or goodness; but we need to remember that we can rely fully on those of Jesus.

- **Eliab (v 28)?** Eliab seems not to consider the possibility that David could have come to the battle in order to win it. He is cross with David for not doing what he (Eliab) thinks he should be doing; he has completely misunderstood who David is and what his God-given role is. Again, it is easy for us to fail to trust Jesus to deliver us from the devil, and/or to grow irritated with him when he fails to do what we think he ought to be doing.

- **Saul (v 33, 38-39)?** Saul shares the world's perspective; he believes that power is found in armour and weapons. He judges based on appearances. Again, we can find it easy either to want Jesus to "fit" with the world's view of what a strong leader should be like, and should say and do; or to be overly impressed by worldly power, and think that the church needs to become more like the world in order to have a chance of surviving or prevailing.

**10. What is the role that God's people *do* play in the story (v 51-53)?** They advance, because the victory is already won, and pursue the Philistines, scattering and plundering them.

**11. APPLY: Read 2 Corinthians 10 v 4-5 and Ephesians 6 v 10-17. What does that look like for God's people today?** The call to action for us is not to take on giants (Jesus has done that for us). It is to

fight, knowing that the decisive victory has already been won in Jesus' death and resurrection. Our job is to plunder our Enemy's camp as we proclaim the victory of Christ and call people to submit to his liberating reign. 2 Corinthians 10 v 4-5 shows us that this means not fighting with worldly weapons/programmes/approaches, but rather by preaching the truth about Jesus Christ wherever we find arguments or worldviews that resist him, either in our own or in others' thoughts. Ephesians 6 v 10-17 encourages us to put on the armour of gospel truth and resist the devil's temptations—we win against him by standing our ground.

**12. APPLY: Why can we joyfully submit to the authority of Christ Jesus in our lives?** Sometimes, living with Christ as Lord can seem to be a price we have to pay to enjoy eternal life, as though it were a burden. But consider David in these chapters. He is a leader of Israel who is chosen by God, filled with God's Spirit, humble in heart, brave enough to face his people's enemies and strengthened by God to defeat them utterly, enabling his people to plunder the Philistines. He brings his people security and safety, as their shepherd. And he is only a shadow of the Lord Jesus. Being ruled by Jesus, the chosen Christ who rules us perfectly and defeats our enemies completely, is (or should be) a wonderful joy.

# 5 1 Samuel 18; 24 – 26
# THE WILDERNESS YEARS

## THE BIG IDEA

The Christian life involves suffering before glory, as it did for David and Jesus. We are to resist temptation in times of "wilderness" as they did, and know that our King's obedience means that we are forgiven when we fail to obey.

## SUMMARY

This study focuses on David's time in the wilderness on the run from Saul. Saul has grown envious, then fearful, then murderous towards David. Despite his anointing and his defeat of Goliath, David does not come straight to the throne. His path to glory involves spending years living on the margins, with no home, facing prejudice and betrayal.

David's wilderness years should reset our expectations of our lives. We should not expect to have a comfortable life because we are a Christian. We should not expect glory without, or before, suffering. Paul said: "We must go through many hardships to enter the kingdom of God" (Acts 14 v 22). Suffering is a must, not an option.

What will help us through our own "wilderness times"? We need to know, as David did, that the kingdom of the Christ will be established by God. That is the content of the encouragement that we need, and need to be willing to hear ourselves and to share with others.

And David's wilderness years are also the pattern of Jesus' time in the wilderness. Both men were tempted three times; both refused to be a compromised king. So both teach us how to live when we are in a "wilderness".

But more than that, Jesus' wilderness time and his refusal to give in to temptation mean two things for us.

First, we have a God who sympathises with us in our trials, because he has been through those trials. And second, we have a Saviour who saves us when we fail in our times of trial. Jesus was faithful in his trials, and he give us his faithfulness. So we are faithful and forgiven in him; and we look to follow him, and cry out to him as we face our own difficult times. The study finishes with these great truths.

## OPTIONAL EXTRA

Twice in these chapters, David is able to come so close to Saul that he can take part of his robe, or his spear and jug, without Saul knowing anything about it. Blindfold one member of your group and sit them on a chair in the middle of the room, with their car keys on the floor by their feet. The rest of the group have to try to take the keys without that person touching them.

## GUIDANCE FOR QUESTIONS

**1. What do you expect the rest of your life to be like? What difference will it make that you are a Christian?** Often, we have an instinctive view that life will be good, and comfortable; we are optimistic for our future on earth. And as Christians, we tend to think that, if anything, life will be even better for us, because we know God is on our side, we can pray to him, we can know we are heading for heaven, etc. In this study, we'll see that we should be expecting hardship, and that many of those hardships will come as a result of our Christian faith.

So you could return to this question after Q7, after the Getting Personal box that follows it, or at the end of the study.

**2. [In 18 v 1-16] Who loves David? Who doesn't love David?**
- Jonathan (Saul's eldest son and heir) loves David (v 1, 3)—the phrase "one in spirit" is literally "knit together".
- The army loves David, both rank and file and the top brass, because he is always victorious (v 5).
- The women of Israel love David—they greet the victorious troops singing of Saul's and David's feats, but they see David's as being greater (v 6-7).
- Everyone loves David! (v 16).
- Your group might point out that, implicitly, God loves David (v 12, 14).
- Saul does NOT love David. Instead, "he was afraid of him" (v 15). See also verses 28-29, where Saul is described as David's enemy. Saul does not only not love David; he comes to hate him.

**3. What reasons are given for Saul's attitude towards David?**
- v 7-9: Saul takes the women's song as a slight. Is is clearly jealous of David, and also feels threatened by him: "what more can he get but the kingdom"?
- v 10: an "evil spirit from God" now plagues Saul. Note: the word "evil" can imply both "wickedness" and "misery". This is probably not a demonic spirit, but rather a spirit that brings misery—a spirit of judgment rather than a spirit that is itself evil. It makes Saul emotionally volatile and paranoid.
- v 12: Saul knows he has been rejected by God; he recognises that the LORD is now "with David".
- v 15: David's success threatens Saul.

**4. Read 1 Samuel 19 v 11-12; 21 v 1; 21 v 10 – 22 v 5; 23 v 15, 24-25. Plot David's escape routes on the map.**
David's route goes from his house in Saul's court in Gibeah (you will need to tell your group this), to Nob; Gath; Adullam; Mizpah; Hereth; and on to Horesh and then Maon.

**5. In chapter 16, God chose David as the next king of his people. In chapter 17, David defeated Israel's greatest enemy. Why is what happens to him next surprising?** We would expect David to be recognised as heir; given the honour he has won through his defeat of Goliath; soon ascend the throne that God has chosen he should sit on; and then to rule powerfully and well. Instead, he becomes a refugee, on the run, constantly having to move around in fear for his life. He may be the man God has chosen as king, but for years he has no home, faces regular attempts to murder him, and is opposed by the most powerful man in Israel. It is hardly the life we would expect God to give his chosen king!

**EXPLORE MORE**
**Read 1 Samuel 18 v 1-4; 19 v 1-3; 20 v 12-17. Jonathan is Saul's son and heir. How is his attitude towards David different to his father's?**
- Far from hating David, he "loved him as himself" (18 v 1). And the giving of his cloak to David in verse 4 is symbolic—back in 15 v 27-28, a cloak represented the kingdom. So Jonathan is giving David the kingdom; taking off his right to be king, and handing it to David.
- Rather than obeying his father's command to kill David, Jonathan warns him (19 v 1-2). His greatest loyalty is to David, not to Saul.
- In 20 v 12-17, Jonathan again pledges himself to David—he promises to protect

David from Saul (v 12-13), and asks David to show kindness to him and his family (v 14). He recognises that God will "cut off" anyone who opposes David (v 15).

**Why is his recognition of David as God's chosen king costly for him personally?** Jonathan is, by hereditary right, Saul's heir. Back in chapter 14, he proved himself a worthy heir. But instead of fighting for the throne by opposing David, Jonathan recognises that God has chosen David to be the next king, and not him. He gives up his own "right" to rule. And he also gives up his relationship with his father (see 20 v 30).

**Jonathan is often held up to us as a model of a good friend. But how is he, much more than this, the model of a good follower of God's King?** He recognises that David has the right to rule, not him. He gives David his loyalty, even at the cost of his relationship with his own father—David comes before Saul in his affections. He gives away any claim to authority over his future, and seeks David's protection for his family. He entrusts his future to David. He is a picture of how we should relate to God's ultimate Christ, the Lord Jesus.

**6. APPLY: So what does David's experience tell us to expect our lives will be like as people chosen by God?** We need to get our expectations right. David suffered before he received glory. He suffered for 20 chapters before gaining the throne. So we should expect to suffer. Too often, we expect to be able to get on in our careers without our faith creating problems for us. Too often, we expect to be able to share our faith without facing opposition. Too often, we expect God to solve our problems and take away our suffering. We are surprised when he lets us stay in the wilderness.

• **What truth could David hang on to in these "wilderness years" (23 v 16-17)?** That he would be king of Israel, and that therefore Saul would not succeed in his efforts to defeat him. The wilderness period would end, and he would rule.

**7. APPLY: When do we find it hardest to remember that the Christian life involves suffering before glory? What happens to our perspective of ourselves and of God when we forget this?** We will all have different parts of our lives where deep down we are expecting or demanding comfort from God, or where we are compromising in our Christian obedience in order to have an easy life. And there will be different times of our life—for instance, when we suffer illness—when it is easy to forget that our lives will see suffering before glory.

If we forget that God does put his people through wilderness times, then we are likely to grow despairing about life, and angry or bitter with God. We may conclude that God is not there or does not love us. We will certainly not know joy in the midst of our suffering.

• **What truths can we hang onto in wilderness times?** We need to hang onto the truths of the gospel! God is in control; and God loves us. He has proved this by sending his Son to die for us (1 John 4 v 10). God will lead us home to glory (Romans 8 v 32). God will not let us be tempted beyond what we can bear (1 Corinthians 10 v 13). Suffering is normal for God's people (Matthew 10 v 16-25; 1 Peter 1 v 6-7). We are on our way to the kingdom (Acts 14 v 22).

Members of your group may be going through hard times as you meet; or you may be enjoying a period of greater comfort. But encourage your group to memorise verses that will help in times of hardship, and to use them not only to encourage themselves, but to encourage others who are in the "wilderness". Essentially, we need to know, as David did, that the kingdom of the Christ will be established by God. That is the content of the encouragement that we need, and need to be willing to hear ourselves, and toshare with others.

**8. Skim-read each chapter [24 – 26]. What is David being tempted to do? What does he do instead?** If you are pushed for time, you could divide your group into three subgroups, and take a chapter each.

- **24 v 1-22 (especially v 3-7, 10-13):** David has the opportunity to kill Saul. His men suggest that this is a God-given opportunity (v 4). He could kill the man who is trying to kill him, and he could be rid of the king who is stopping him ruling God's people. He could grab the kingdom. Instead, David creeps up and cuts off the corner of Saul's robe (v 4)—and even then, he is "conscience-stricken", because he has done this to "the anointed of the LORD" (v 6—remember, the robe is a symbol of the kingdom). David refuses to do the wrong thing (v 11). He refuses to take God's place and act as the judge and punisher (v 12). Instead, he will wait for God to give him the kingdom.

- **25 v 1-44 (especially v 21-34):** David is sorely tempted to kill Nabal and all his men (v 22), in revenge for Nabal paying "[him] back evil for good" (v 21). David is extremely angry.
But in the end, David listens to Abigail, Nabal's wife, who points out that God is protecting him (v 29), and that he does not want "the staggering burden of

needless bloodshed" on his conscience (v 31). Again, David lets God be the judge and avenger, and does not take that role for himself (v 33).

- **26 v 1-25 (especially v 7-11):** Again, David is tempted to force God's hand. This time, he would not even need to kill Saul himself (v 8).
But instead, David stops Abishai from killing Saul (v 9). He imagines a number of scenarios for Saul's future (v 10)—an untimely death, a natural death or a violent death in battle. God will achieve his purposes and bring justice; David will not tell God how he should or must act, or take that decision into his own hands.

**9. Imagine David had given in to each temptation. What kind of a king would he have been by the time he ruled over Israel?** He would have a been a compromised christ—a murderer, who had sought comfort instead of obedience, who had disrespected God's anointing, and who had killed men out of his own anger at being slighted. He would have been a king who saw himself as the judge, rather than God; who avenged his enemies himself, rather than trusting God to bring justice and vindication in his own timing.

**10. Read Luke 4 v 1-13. What was Jesus, David's greater son, being tempted to do in the wilderness? What did he do instead?** Christ Jesus also faced a three-fold test in the wilderness:
- To use his power to serve himself and make himself comfortable (v 3)—instead, he obeyed God's word, and refused to take a shortcut through wilderness suffering.
- To gain supreme power and honour without having to go through hardship, by worshipping the devil instead of obeying

his Father (v 5-7). Instead, he obeyed God's word, even though this would take him to the cross before it brought him to glory and power.

- To prove himself and his status as God's Son—to enjoy vindication and public affirmation (v 9-11). Instead, he obeyed God's word, and did not "put the Lord your God to the test".

- **Imagine Jesus had given into each temptation. What kind of a King would he be?** A horribly compromised king, who put his own interests first, who worshipped the devil in order to enjoy power without cost, and who gloried in his own position and reputation in a proud way.

**11. APPLY: What temptations do we face when life seems particularly difficult, or unfair, or to be going wrong?** There are many. Here are a few:

- Despair with ourselves
- Envy towards others
- Bitterness towards God
- Compromise with sin (we justify sinning a little because life is so hard, or it seems impossible to resist, or we are tired)

- **What do David and Jesus teach us about how to resist those temptations?** We have already seen we need to get our expectations right. David teaches us to trust in God to right wrongs, judge injustice, and vindicate his people. He also teaches us to trust in God's timing in all these things; not to force God's hand by taking matters into our own hands. He also teaches us not to seek ways out of suffering, but to remain faithful and obedient in it.

The Lord Jesus' example is one which, again, refuses to take an easy, compromised way out. And he shows us how we should know, and remember, and live by the word of God as we seek to live rightly in hard times.

**12. APPLY: As we have seen, "we do not have a high priest who is unable to feel sympathy for our weaknesses, but we have one who has been tempted in every way, just as we are—yet he did not sin" (Hebrews 4 v 15). How should this truth affect:**

- **your view of Jesus?** Jesus did not go straight to being crowned. He experienced problems and pain and then he experienced a horrendous death. He was not some super-human, floating easily through his years on earth, impervious to the kinds of tensions and issues that we face each day. And so he always understands. He always knows what it is like for us. We can bring our problems to Jesus.

Yet he also "did not sin". As we consider our own struggles, and our own failings in them, we should be all the more amazed that Jesus faced all that we face, and more, and never once disobeyed God. He is wonderful.

- **your response to any struggles you are facing?** We should not be surprised. We should not compromise, and we can never excuse compromise, because Jesus faced those things and did not sin. And in those struggles, we can and should speak to and rely on Jesus. He knows what it is like; he does not forget us. When we are in the wilderness, it can never be more than he experienced. And since he came through the wilderness, our suffering can never be more than he can help us with, and help us through.

# 6

## 1 Samuel 28; 30 –31
# THE KING IS DEAD...

## THE BIG IDEA

Jesus is the presence of God and the bringer of peace with God, because he is the King God sent to give to his people, just as David did. We have no need to look anywhere else for a loving presence or reassurance.

## SUMMARY

Through the last five chapters, the action switches between David and Saul. The events happen at the same time, and we see them from the two men's perspectives.

David has ended up living in Philistine territory (27 v 1-4). Now he faces fighting against Israel (28 v 1-2). Saul is facing the invading Philistine armies in terror (v 4-5). Though circumstances enable David to leave the Philistine army, he finds on his return to his base in Ziklag that all his men's families have been taken by Amalekite raiders (29 v 1 – 30 v 6). Both men face powerful enemies and the prospect of defeat.

Saul enquires of the LORD, but there is no answer (28 v 6). So he decides to visit a medium to connect with Samuel, who has now died (v 7-11). Though "successful", the only word he receives from Samuel is a word of judgment. He has been rejected by God—and he will die the next day (v 16-19). In the end, Saul kills himself on the battlefield (31 v 4). He has always been the master of his own downfall, and is so even in death.

David, meanwhile, enquires of the LORD, and is answered—not least because he has the priest and the ephod (30 v 7-8—see Explore More section). He finds the Amalekites, rescues the women and children, and takes a great deal of plunder (v 16-20). He

then shows the kind of king he will be by distributing the plunder generously among men who have not fought and elders from the tribe of Judah (v 21-31). The book (which is really only the first half of the book of Samuel) closes with Saul dead, and God's chosen king ready to rule.

**Note:** There is a more detailed discussion on the issue of mediums and spiritualists in *1 Samuel For You*, pages 184-187.

## OPTIONAL EXTRA

(1) Play "Name the successor". Choose five or six leaders from your nation's past (monarchs, presidents, etc), and then challenge the group to tell you who succeeded them.

(2) At the end of the study, continue the story by reading 2 Samuel 1 v 1 – 5 v 5 (David becoming king of all Israel) or all the way to 7 v 29 (God's promises to David).

## GUIDANCE FOR QUESTIONS

**1. Why do people try to contact the dead?** For a variety of reasons—discuss this without feeling the need to come up with a single answer. But perhaps (as suggested in the Study Guide, Q6) it comes down to one of two broad motives. First, people go to mediums because they cannot bear to live without someone they have lost—without that person, there seems no purpose to life, so they will do anything to re-establish contact. Second, because they want reassurance about their future, or what lies beyond the grave.

**2. Why does Saul end up consulting a medium (28 v 5-7, 15)?** He is afraid because he is facing a Philistine army (v 5). Though Saul has faced and conquered Philistine armies before, this time he knows it is different, because "God has departed from [him]" (v 15).

Saul seeks answers or guidance from God, but "the LORD did not answer him" (v 6). So, terrified and desperate, Saul "enquire[s] of" a medium—someone who claims to be able to connect to the dead (v 7).

**EXPLORE MORE**
**In verse 6, what does God not do for Saul?** He does not answer Saul when Saul seeks guidance from him.
**Read 1 Samuel 30 v 7-8. What does God do for David? What does David have brought to him, and by whom?** David faces a similar situation to Saul; a raiding army has brought catastrophe. But God speaks to David, answering his questions (v 8). He does this after David has Abiathar, the priest, bring him the ephod (a linen cloth the priest wore, on which were the Urim and Thummim, objects used to discern guidance from God).
**Read 1 Samuel 22 v 6-23. Why do Abiathar and the ephod end up with David, rather than with King Saul?** This event took place some years before, towards the beginning of Saul's campaign to kill David. David had sheltered with the priests at Nob, so Saul had them executed. Only one escaped—Abiathar. He fled to David, taking the ephod with him (see 23 v 6). David ends up with the means to hear from God because Saul had killed the priests.
**Saul had literally silenced the priests. What is the tragic irony of 28 v 6?** In killing the priests because they had sheltered David, Saul had extinguished his ability to hear from God. Now, when he needs to hear from the LORD, he cannot. Saul has replaced the priests and ephod—a way to

hear from God himself—with a medium—a means prohibited by God.

**3. And what is the message Samuel brings to Saul (28 v 16-19)?** It is nothing new, but a reiteration of what Samuel has previously told Saul. The LORD has departed from Saul (v 16); he has torn the kingdom from him and given it to David (v 17); and he has done this because Saul failed to trust and obey him (v 18). The only new information is a detail; that the next day, Saul will be defeated and he will die (v 19).

• **How does Saul recognise Samuel (v 14)? Why is this significant (see 15 v 27-28)?** By his robe. This is the robe which, the last time these two men met, Saul had ripped as he tried to cling to his kingdom in the face of Samuel's message of God's rejection. Samuel's robe is a reminder that Saul has been rejected.

**4. Read Isaiah 8 v 19. What should God's people not do, and what should they do?** Don't consult those who seek to get in touch with the spirit world or the dead. Do enquire of God. Why go to dead people when you can hear from the living God?

**5. Read Matthew 28 v 18-20; John 20 v 19, 26. Where do we find the true presence of God and a real reassurance from God?** Jesus is the presence of God, with us (Matthew 28 v 18-20). He is the one with all authority, risen from the dead, and his last words in Matthew are: "Surely I am with you always, to the very end of the age". Through his Spirit, God's Son is present with us.

And Jesus brings us reassurance from God. He tells his flawed disciples, who had deserted him and were cowering behind a locked door: "Peace be with you!" In his death and resurrection, Jesus has reconciled us to God, with whom we had been enemies (Colossians 1 v 21-22). There is nothing better than having God as our friend, and nothing can take that away. Jesus says: "Peace" to his people. It is a wonderful reassurance about our status before God, and our future destination.

- **How is what we hear from Jesus very different from what Saul heard from Samuel?** Samuel, God's prophet, has a word for Saul, and it is this: *War*. The LORD will deliver Saul and Israel into the hands of the Philistines. God has rejected him and departed from him. That is all Saul hears. We, on the other hand, are told: *Peace*. The LORD is with us, by his Spirit, and has defeated all our enemies. The one who speaks to us from beyond the grave, the risen Jesus, tells us the opposite of what Samuel told Saul.

**6. APPLY: Why does knowing the Lord Jesus mean we do not need to do either [seek the presence of someone from beyond the grave, or seek reassurance about life beyond the grave]?** Because:
1. We know God is with us, through Jesus.
2. If we know Jesus, he becomes more precious to us than anyone else, and is our greatest love. We'll grieve the loss of a loved one, but we won't feel there is no point going on unless we continue to have contact with them, because they were never the centre of our lives or the primary source of our joy—God is.
3. We do not need to wonder what has happened to our loved ones. The Bible is quite clear what happens when people die. And we do not need to find out what the future will be for us—we can

know for sure that we are at peace with God and will live with him eternally. We already know all we need to about life beyond the grave.

- **We might not use a medium; but how is it possible to seek a loving presence, or some reassurance, in places other than in God's Son?** *Presence:* Grieving people might grow a habit of speaking to a loved one who has died as though they are still there. Or, we might seek God's presence outside the way in which God communicates to us—through his Son's word, and by his Spirit's work in making it alive to us. We may seek to "conjure up" God's closer presence through a particular style of singing, or emotional state. Or we may seek to hear from God somewhere other than in the Bible (often because we don't like what God is saying in the Bible). *Reassurance:* We might seek to control our immediate future via technology or wealth, reassuring ourselves that we are OK because we are secure, or have money as an "insurance policy". We might base our assurance for our eternal future on our performance in life, rather than on Jesus' finished work on the cross.

**7. What does David find in Ziklag (v 3-6)?** The Amalekites have attacked the town and taken their women and children away. Encourage your group to picture the scene; David and his men returning to the deathly quiet town, and the truth dawning on them; every single member of every single family has been taken.
**How is this a crisis for his leadership?** David's men talk of stoning him (v 6). They had entrusted everything to him, and now they have lost everything. David faces not only losing his authority, but his life.

**8. APPLY: What does David's reaction**

teach us about how to respond to a crisis in a godly way?

- **v 6b:** We find strength in the LORD our God. In verse 4, David "had no strength left" because of his grief. But where our strength fails, God's takes over. Take your group to 23 v 16-17 to see what this means. There, Jonathan: "helped [David] to find strength in God". How? By reminding him of God's promises to him. When we face a crisis, we need to remind ourselves of God's promises to us: that he is in control, that he cares for us, that he has sent his King to rescue us, and will send his King to dwell with us.

- **v 7-8 (Hint: the ephod was the way God had given his people to find his wisdom):** We turn to God's word to seek guidance from him. In a crisis, it is easy to turn in on ourselves, either in despair or self-reliance. We ignore God, and then wonder why he seems distant. David turned to God for help and wisdom; we can do the same. But where David needed to turn to the priest and ephod, we turn to God's words in Scripture.

**9. When David pursues the Amalekites, what is the end result (v 17-20)?** David is victorious—only 400 of the Amalekites get away (v 17). Everything is recovered (v 18-19). And his reputation is restored—the men who had wanted to stone him now recognise the plunder is his (v 20).

**10. What kind of king does David show himself to be in v 21-31?** Two hundred of David's men were too exhausted to fight the Amalekites. Understandably, the men who did fight feel that no share of the plunder should go those who did not help (v 22). But David proves himself to be a generous king who dispenses gifts to those who do not

deserve them (v 23-25). And he also shares the plunder with the elders of his tribe, Judah (v 26-30). Samuel had warned that a king like those of the nations would *take* (8 v 10-17). Here is the king God has chosen and given to his people—he *gives* to the ones left behind and *gives* to Judah's elders.

- **How does Jesus show himself to be this kind of king, to a far greater extent than David?** Jesus is the ultimate giving King. He gave his life so that he might give us his presence through his Spirit, his relationship with his Father, his gifts to build up his people, his kingdom for eternity, and so on.

**11. Saul has been the architect of his own downfall throughout his reign. How is the manner of his death a fitting end for him?** The Philistines did not remove Saul from God's favour, and neither did David. Saul did it, through his disobedience and lack of true repentance. Now, the Philistines do not remove him from his throne or from his life, and neither does David. He does it himself.

**12. APPLY: How has this history of Saul and David shown you:**
- **how you are tempted to choose the wrong kind of ruler?**
- **how great it is to live under the rule of God's chosen King?**
- **how to respond to difficulty as David did?**

You could ask each person to write something down for each part of this question, before sharing responses. People will, of course, have been encouraged and challenged in different ways by the Spirit as you have studied 1 Samuel together.

# DIG DEEPER INTO 1 SAMUEL

In *1 Samuel For You*, Tim brings his trademark clarity, grace and insight to the book of 1 Samuel. Written for Christians of every age and stage, whether new believers or pastors and teachers, each title in the series takes a detailed look at a part of the Bible in a readable, relevant way.

Find out more at:
**www.thegoodbook.com/for-you**
**www.thegoodbook.co.uk/for-you**

## A small selection from the Good Book Guide series...

### OLD TESTAMENT

**2 Samuel: The fall and rise of the King** *By Tim Chester*   6 studies
ISBN: 9781784982195

**Ruth: Poverty and plenty**
*By Tim Chester*   4 studies
ISBN: 9781905564910

### NEW TESTAMENT

**Mark 1–8: The coming King**
*By Tim Chester*   10 studies
ISBN: 9781904889281

**Romans 1–7: The gift of God**
*By Timothy Keller*   7 studies.
ISBN: 9781908762924

**James: Genuine faith**
*By Sam Allberry*   6 studies
ISBN: 9781910307816

### TOPICAL

**Work: Making work work**
*By Marcus Nodder*   8 studies
ISBN: 9781908762894

**Promises kept: Bible overview**
*By Carl Laferton*   9 studies
ISBN: 9781908317933

Visit your friendly neighbourhood website to see the full range, and to download samples
• **US:** www.thegoodbook.com • **UK & Europe:** www.thegoodbook.co.uk •
• **Australia:** www.thegoodbook.com.au • **New Zealand:** www.thegoodbook.co.nz •

**BIBLICAL | RELEVANT | ACCESSIBLE**

At The Good Book Company, we are dedicated to helping Christians and local churches grow. We believe that God's growth process always starts with hearing clearly what he has said to us through his timeless word—the Bible.

Ever since we opened our doors in 1991, we have been striving to produce Bible-based resources that bring glory to God. We have grown to become an international provider of user-friendly resources to the Christian community, with believers of all backgrounds and denominations using our books, Bible studies, devotionals, evangelistic resources, and DVD-based courses.

We want to equip ordinary Christians to live for Christ day by day, and churches to grow in their knowledge of God, their love for one another, and the effectiveness of their outreach.

Call us for a discussion of your needs or visit one of our local websites for more information on the resources and services we provide.

Your friends at The Good Book Company

thegoodbook.com | thegoodbook.co.uk
thegoodbook.com.au | thegoodbook.co.nz
thegoodbook.co.in